Centering Diverse Bodyminds in Critical Qualitative Inquiry

Centering Diverse Bodyminds in Critical Qualitative Inquiry directly responds to the call for engaging in a new critical qualitative inquiry with consideration to issues related to power, privilege, voice, identity, and agency, while examining the hegemonic power of ableism and ableist epistemologies.

The contributing authors of this edited volume advance qualitative methods and methodological discussions to a place where disability embodiment and the lived experience of disability are potential sources of method and methodological advancement. Accordingly, this book centers disability, and, in so doing, examines methodological challenges related to normative and ableist assumptions of doing qualitative research. The range of chapters included highlights how there is no singular answer to questions about qualitative method and methodology; rather, the centering of diverse bodyminds complicates the normative desire to create method/methodology that is "standard," versus thinking about method and methodology as fluid, emerging, and disruptive.

As an interdisciplinary text on critical qualitative research and disability studies with an international appeal, *Centering Diverse Bodyminds in Critical Qualitative Inquiry* is valuable for graduate level students and academics within a broad range of fields including critical qualitative research methodologies and methods, disability studies, cultural studies, discourse studies, education, sociology, and psychology. Disciplines that engage in the teaching of qualitative research methodologies and methods, particularly those that foreground critical qualitative research perspectives, will also find the book appealing.

Jessica Nina Lester, PhD is an associate professor of inquiry methodology in the School of Education at Indiana University, Bloomington. Much of her scholarship focuses on methodological concerns at the intersection of discourse and conversation analysis and disability studies. She has most recently published in journals such as *Qualitative Inquiry*, *Qualitative Research in Psychology*, and *Discourse Studies*. Most recently, she co-authored a book with Sage publications titled *Doing Qualitative Research in a Digital World*.

Emily A. Nusbaum, PhD currently teaches at Mills College and University of San Diego. She has worked in teacher education and special education departments, has taught undergraduate and graduate level courses in disability studies in education and interdisciplinary disability studies, as well as qualitative research methods. Her research focuses on the advancement of critical, qualitative research through the centering of disability and disabled researchers, the ideology of inclusive education, and the experiences of post-secondary students who identify as disabled. Emily is invested in supporting individuals and families in accessing general education and higher education environments, which they have historically been denied access to.

Developing Traditions in Qualitative Inquiry
Series Editors: Jasmine Brooke Ulmer and James Salvo
Wayne State University

The Developing Traditions in Qualitative Inquiry series invites scholars to share novel and innovative work in accessible ways, ways such that others might discover their own paths, too. In acknowledging who and what have respectively influenced our work along the way, this series encourages thoughtful engagements with approaches to inquiry – ones that are situated within ongoing scholarly conversations. Neither stuck in tradition nor unaware of it, volumes make new scholarly contributions to qualitative inquiry that attend to what's shared across disciplines and methodological approaches. By design, qualitative inquiry is a tradition of innovation in and of itself, one aimed at the target of justice.

From multiple perspectives and positionalities, concise volumes in this series (20,000 to 50,000 words) strengthen and grow the qualitative community by developing inquiry traditions as they should be developed: inclusively, diversely, and together.

For more information about the series or proposal guidelines, please write the Series Editors at jasmine.ulmer@wayne.edu and salvo@wayne.edu.

Other volumes in this series include:

Shared and Collaborative Practice in Qualitative Inquiry
Tiny Revolutions
Jasmine Brooke Ulmer

Writing and Unrecognized Academic Labor
The Rejected Manuscript
James M. Salvo

Centering Diverse Bodyminds in Critical Qualitative Inquiry
Edited by Jessica Nina Lester & Emily A. Nusbaum

For a full list of titles in this series, please visit www.routledge.com/ Developing-Traditions-in-Qualitative-Inquiry/book-series/DTQI

Centering Diverse Bodyminds in Critical Qualitative Inquiry

Edited by Jessica Nina Lester
and Emily A. Nusbaum

LONDON AND NEW YORK

First published 2021
by Routledge
2 Park Square, Milton Park, Abingdon, Oxon OX14 4RN

and by Routledge
605 Third Avenue, New York, NY 10158

Routledge is an imprint of the Taylor & Francis Group, an informa business

British Library Cataloguing-in-Publication Data
A catalogue record for this book is available from the British Library

Library of Congress Cataloging-in-Publication Data
Names: Lester, Jessica Nina, editor. | Nusbaum, Emily A., editor.
Title: Centering diverse bodyminds in critical qualitative inquiry / edited
    by Jessica Nina Lester & Emily A. Nusbaum.
Description: Abingdon, Oxon ; New York, NY : Routledge, 2021. | Includes
    bibliographical references and index. | Identifiers: LCCN 2021004045
    (print) | LCCN 2021004046 (ebook) | ISBN 9780367470869 (hbk) |
    ISBN 9781032041254 (pbk) | ISBN 9781003033264 (ebk)
Subjects: LCSH: Disability studies. | People with disabilities. | Qualitative
    research. | Social sciences—Research.
Classification: LCC HV1568.2 .C343 2021 (print) | LCC HV1568.2
    (ebook) | DDC 362.4072/1—dc23
LC record available at https://lccn.loc.gov/2021004045
LC ebook record available at https://lccn.loc.gov/2021004046

ISBN: 978-0-367-47086-9 (hbk)
ISBN: 978-1-032-04125-4 (pbk)
ISBN: 978-1-003-03326-4 (ebk)

Typeset in Times New Roman
by Apex CoVantage, LLC

Contents

Author biographies

Brianna Dickens is a PhD candidate in special education and disability studies at Syracuse University. They teach courses to preserve special education students, as well as graduate level courses related to disability and theory. Brianna works on research teams that center the perspectives of disabled people and expand who is a researcher, how research is done, and how it is disseminated. Brianna is an autistic self-advocate who works to bring together their neurodiverse ways of being, their education, and research training to critically analyze current educational systems and structures to supporting educators in both K-12 and higher education to think about pedagogy and practice in ways that center multiply marginalized students and support a more just and equitable educational system.

Alison L. Grittner is a PhD candidate in the Faculty of Social Work at the University of Calgary. Previously educated in architecture, fine arts, and history, her transdisciplinary approach involves working alongside vulnerable communities to reimagine, codesign, and reconstruct everyday environments towards equity, empowerment, and dignity. Her award-winning praxis focuses on developing community-based knowledge of socio-spatial inequity and translating that awareness into action and intervention via the built environment. Her longstanding work with the disability community led to her creation of the RAD Renovations program at Accessible Housing Calgary: a design, construction, and advocacy program for low-income disabled persons. This ongoing program has forged hundreds of new home environments designed for disabled persons' unique bodies, based on their lived experiences. Underpinning her work is the belief that multisensory and arts-based ways of knowing are a potent and untapped means of exploring emplaced experiences and spatial justice.

Stephanie L. Kerschbaum, PhD is an associate professor of English at the University of Washington, where she directs the Expository Writing

Program and teaches courses in writing studies and disability studies. Her first book, *Toward a New Rhetoric of Difference*, was awarded the 2015 Advancement of Knowledge Award from the Conference on College Composition and Communication. She is the co-editor of *Negotiating Disability: Disclosure and Higher Education* and has published essays in *Rhetoric Review, Disability Society Quarterly, College Composition and Communication, enculturation, Pedagogy, Composition Forum, Research in the Teaching of English*, and several essay collections.

Estée Klar holds a PhD in critical disability studies from York University. Her dissertation, *Neurodiversity in Relation: an artistic intraethnography*, is a collaborative work with her non-speaking autistic son/poet, Adam Wolfond, and The A Collective (recently renamed Dis assembly) based in Toronto of which she is a co-founder, or as she prefers to say, anti-director. Dis assembly is a neurodiverse artistic collective that thinks about the techniques and conditions that support neurodiversity. This work shifts research creation and rethinks the neurodiversity, contribution, and value, and questions the hegemony of intelligibility and instrumentality through relational-processual artistic work. Estée also holds master's degrees in fine art and critical disability studies. She is the founder of the former Autism Acceptance Project (2006–16) and its subsequent artistic-activist events, and the original blogger at The Joy of Autism (2004–8). She is an artist and filmmaker and her work with Adam can be seen at www.esteerelation.com. New work from the collective: www.dis-assembly.ca.

Jessica Nina Lester, PhD is an associate professor of inquiry methodology in the School of Education at Indiana University, Bloomington. Much of her scholarship focuses on methodological concerns at the intersection of discourse and conversation analysis and disability studies. She has most recently published in journals such as *Qualitative Inquiry, Qualitative Research in Psychology*, and *Discourse Studies*. Most recently, she co-authored a book with Sage publications titled *Doing Qualitative Research in a Digital World.*

Emily A. Nusbaum, PhD currently teaches at Mills College and the University of San Diego. She has worked in teacher education and special education departments, has taught undergraduate and graduate level courses in disability studies in education and interdisciplinary disability studies, as well as qualitative research methods. Her research focuses on the advancement of critical, qualitative research through the centering of disability and disabled researchers, the ideology of inclusive education, and the experiences of post-secondary students who identify as disabled. Emily is invested in supporting individuals and families in accessing general education and higher education environments, which they have historically been denied access to.

Holly Pearson, PhD is a visiting assistant professor whose scholarship utilizes an interdisciplinary approach in exploring and addressing the disconnect between institutional diversity, disability, access, inclusion, equity, and socio-spatial justice in higher education. As a scholar who embodies multiple marginalized identities (Deaf/disabled, queer, transracial adoptee), her lived experiences and advanced interdisciplinary training in sociology and social justice education offer insights of the critical issues surrounding higher education in terms of intersectional access and equity, in particular for multiply marginalized communities. Besides academia, she dreams about new ways to approach food, working out, doing yoga, and figuring out ways to entwine her passion of architecture, design, food, and social justice into forms of community space(s) of compassion and resilience.

Kathleen C. Sitter, PhD is the Canada Research Chair in Multisensory Storytelling Research and Knowledge Translation and an associate professor in the Faculty of Social Work at the University of Calgary. Kathleen has worked with a variety of adults and youth in the areas of disability, where her work primarily focuses on sexual health, access, arts and health, and participatory health research. Her research has been published in national and international journals and supported through local, provincial, and national grants. Kathleen's scholarship also involves creative forms of academic research, such as cartoon abstracts, social media exhibitions, and participatory videos. This includes over 200 arts-based participatory works and over 100 juried screenings and instillations. Currently, Kathleen's research focus involves multisensory engaged research and knowledge translation. In partnership with Calgary Scope Society, Kathleen is currently working alongside disabled youth activists exploring transition experiences into community-living, employment, and post-secondary education.

Adam Wolfond is a non-speaking autistic artist, poet, and presenter attending Ryerson University. He is the co-founder of The A Collective (renamed Dis assembly) in Toronto where he also works in visual art and poetry. Wolfond also collaborated on the PhD dissertation *Neurodiversity in Relation: Movement, S/Pace, Collaboration* with Estée Klar at York University in Toronto, Canada. His collaborative exhibition film installation *S/Pace* at Critical Distance Centre for Curators in 2019 was part of the *Access is Love and Love is Complicated* group exhibition. His other film and art work can be viewed at *esteerelation.com* and dis-assembly.ca. Wolfond is interested in the movement of language (which he refers to as "languaging") and expression, and how neurotypical language forms delimit neurodiverse expression. His poetry has been featured on poets. org. His chapbooks of poetry *In Way of Music Water Answers Toward Questions Other Than What Is Autism* is available through his publisher, Unrestricted Editions.

Alice Wong is a disabled activist, media maker, and consultant. She has a MS in medical sociology and worked at the University of California, San Francisco as a staff research associate for over 10 years. During that time she worked on various qualitative research projects and co-authored online curricula for the Community Living Policy Center, a Rehabilitation Research and Training Center funded by the National Institute on Disability, Independent Living, and Rehabilitation Research. Currently, Alice is the Director of the Disability Visibility Project, an online community dedicated to creating, sharing, and amplifying disability media and culture and host of Disability Visibility podcast. Alice is the Editor of *Disability Visibility: First-Person Stories from the Twenty-First Century* (June 30, 2020), an anthology of essays by disabled people by Vintage Books. You can find her on Twitter: @SFdirewolf/ @DisVisibility; website: https://disabilityvisibilityproject.com/.

Acknowledgments

There are many individuals who have made the development and production of this book possible. First, we wish to offer our gratitude to the contributing authors. Each author has produced a timely, provocative, and long overdue illustration of the need for and importance of *centering* disability in qualitative research. Second, we are grateful to Drs. James Salvo and Jasmine Brooke Ulmer, the series editors, for encouraging and inviting us to develop this volume. Third, we appreciate the support of the editorial team at Routledge in bringing this book to production. Finally, we are grateful to the anonymous reviewers who served to push and extend the ideas presented in this volume.

1 An introduction to *Centering Diverse Bodyminds in Critical Qualitative Inquiry*

Jessica Nina Lester and Emily A. Nusbaum

This edited volume, *Centering Diverse Bodyminds in Critical Qualitative Inquiry*, includes a collection of six chapters that function in various ways as a direct response to the call for engaging in a new critical qualitative inquiry (Flick, 2017). In 2018, we co-edited a special issue in *Qualitative Inquiry* that worked to *center* disability in critical qualitative research (Kerschbaum & Price, 2017), positioning the articles included within it as a direct response to the call for a new critical qualitative inquiry (Lester & Nusbaum, 2018). More particularly, Denzin (2017) stated that "this is a historical present that cries out for emancipatory visions, for visions that inspire transformative inquiries, and for inquiries that can provide the moral authority to move people to struggle and resist oppression" (p. 8). Building on this, this volume *centers* disability, as the contributing authors collectively consider methodological and theoretical issues related to power, privilege, voice, identity, and agency. In so doing, the often taken-for-granted and even normalized hegemonic power of ableism and epistemologies of ableism are critiqued and unpacked. Similar to Goodley, we note here that foregrounding disability functions as a "platform or plateau through which to think through, act, resist, relate, communicate, engage with one another against the hybridized forms of oppression and discrimination that so often do not speak singularly of disability" (Goodley, 2013, p. 641).

In this way, this volume extends conversation about disability and qualitative research practice by centering multiply marginalized knowledge production and ideas related to *doing* qualitative research and developing qualitative methodologies in ways that orient to disability embodiment and the lived experience of disability as potential sources of method and methodological advancement. Such an orientation stands in stark contrast to the view of "disabled people" are being primarily "research informants who have little say about the intellectual purposes their input serves which may lead to underuse of disabled people's experiential expertise" (Mogendorff,

2017, p. np). Indeed, through centering disability, all of the contributing authors examine a range of methodological challenges related to normative and ableist assumptions of doing qualitative research. The range of chapters included highlights how there is no singular "answer" to questions about qualitative method and methodology – but rather the centering of diverse bodyminds complicates the normative desire to create method/ methodology that is "standard," versus thinking about method and methodology as fluid, emerging, and disruptive – as the disabled bodymind (Price, 2014) requires.

In this brief introductory chapter, we situate the volume and overview its contours. To do so, we first begin by offering a very abbreviated discussion of critical qualitative inquiry to better place the discussion of centering disability within it. We then move to present the structure and organization of the book, highlighting key ideas from each of the individual chapters. We conclude by pointing to how this volume might serve to reach a diverse audience – one not solely situated within the ivory tower. Rather, we emphasize how the writing within this volume functions to underscore grassroots wisdom and the often taken for granted knowledge about *doing* qualitative research and *being* qualitative researchers.

Engaging possibilities: critical qualitative inquiry and disability

Ulmer (2020) reminded scholars of the importance of knowing well the inquiry traditions that they one day might ultimately come to critique. She noted that if we do not take the necessary time to study the traditions that we ultimately pivot away from, we can "end up disturbing inquiry traditions that we may not yet grasp, as we did not first become properly acquainted" (p. 454). Informed by her ideas, we begin the chapter by offering an overview of critical qualitative inquiry, albeit brief, in an attempt to sketch out a re-imagining of critical qualitative inquiry that is drawn with care and caution. In doing so, we hope to call for a refusal to settle for doing critical qualitative inquiry as it has always been done. Here, we lean into Ulmer's reminder that:

> Proceeding with care, caution, and appreciation does not mean declining to proceed at all. Unsettling traditions can offer a thoughtful balance between conservation and revolution – between stewardship and change – between rotation and return. In removing sediments at the bottom of the riverbed, the unsettling of traditions can encourage life anew. It can replenish and regenerate while also refusing to settle.
>
> (p. 456)

Thus, with a nod of gratitude for what has come before, we begin by unpacking some of what critical qualitative inquiry is, while pointing also to what it might become.

Critical qualitative inquiry

Critical theorists and scholars have long offered incisive critiques of the discourses, practices, and structures that reinforce and reify systemic inequities. As a social philosophy, critical theory has been shaped by Marxist ideas broadly and the Frankfurt School more particularly. From Horkheimer to Gramsci to Habermas, among many others, critical theory has been leveraged to examine and make explicit how humans operate and struggle for power, with inequalities often being visible based on race, ethnicity, socioeconomic differences, disability, gender, sexual orientation, etc. (Giroux, 1982; Kilgore, 2001). Carspecken (1996) noted that "'criticalists'... are all concerned about social inequalities" and "share a concern with social theory and some of the basic issues it has struggled with since the nineteenth century. These include the nature of social structure, power, culture, and human agency" (p. 3). Lincoln, Lynham, and Guba (2018) noted that critical researchers generally aim to change some aspect of an existing structure, policy, or practice, with *change* being foregrounded. Further, they noted that the position of a researcher is often one of activist, with an eye toward "producing a fair society through social justice" (p. 125).

Similarly, Kinchloe and McLaren (1994) defined a "criticalist" in the following way:

> a researcher or theorist who attempts to use her or his work as a form of social or cultural criticism and who accepts certain basic assumptions: that all thought is fundamentally mediated by power relations which are socially and historically constituted; that facts can never be isolated from the domain of values or removed from some form of ideological inscription; that the relationship between concept and object and signifier and signified is never stable or fixed and is often mediated by the social relations of capitalist production and consumption; that language is central to the formation of subjectivity (conscious and unconscious awareness); that certain groups in any society are privileged over others and, although the reasons for this privileging may vary widely, the oppression which characterizes contemporary societies is most forcefully reproduced when subordinates accept their social status as natural, necessary or inevitable; that oppression has many faces and that focusing on only one at the expense of others (e.g. class oppression versus racism) often elides the interconnections among them; and finally,

> *that mainstream research practices are generally, although most often*
> *unwittingly, implicated in the reproduction of systems of class, race*
> *and gender oppression.*
>
> (*emphasis added*, pp. 139–140)

Here, Kinchloe and McLaren highlighted the role that non-critical research methodology and methods play in reproducing the status quo. A *critical qualitative methodology*, while a relatively recent development (see Carspecken, 1996, for more details related to this), is one that asks questions about *what could be* (Thomas, 1993), including how research paradigms, methodologies, and methods are being conceptualized and applied.

Moreover, in the historical present, the place and conceptualization of critical qualitative methodology has been revisited. For instance, in the recent *Handbook of Qualitative Research*, Denzin and Lincoln (2017) asked: "what is the role of critical qualitative research in a historical present when the need for social justice has never been greater?" (p. 1). They noted that "this is a historical present that cries out for emancipatory visions, for visions that inspire people to struggle and resist oppression" (p. 1). In 2017, Flick (2017) edited a special issue of *Qualitative Inquiry* that focused on engaging the potential challenges and urgent need for a new critical qualitative inquiry. Flick outlined a multi-level approach for engaging what he referred to as new critical qualitative inquiry – one which is relevant to society. These levels include: 1) inquiry being centered on social problems that often include "vulnerable groups" and "hard-to-reach groups" (p. 4); 2) a researcher being critical of the very methodologies and methods used for an empirical study; and 3) a commitment to continuing with qualitative research despite the challenges noted in the first and second levels. Notably, Denzin (2017), a contributor to Flick's special issue, incisively argued that there has "never been a greater need for interpretive, critical, performative qualitative research that matters in the lives of those who daily experience social injustice" (p. 8).

Some scholars have also argued for a critiquing of the "critical" and have offered in response to this critique a postcritical ethnography (Noblit, Flores, & Murillo, 2004). While beyond the scope of this chapter, we suggest a postcritical qualitative perspective is useful to our call for the centering of disability in critical qualitative research, specifically given its explicit commitment to studying systemic inequities and power, practicing reflexivity, and critiquing static representations of culture and claims of objective truth. Like critical qualitative researchers, postcritical researchers also ask questions about *what could be* and reject claims of realism and objectivity, with the "post" referring to postmodern and poststructural work that "rejects a claim to objective knowledge" (Noblit et al., 2004, p. 18).

Disability and critical qualitative research

What often has been (perhaps unintentionally) omitted in much of the methodological writing around critical and postcritical qualitative inquiry is the importance and generative possibilities found in closely attending to how to design critical qualitative research that centers disabled people and communities. Historically, critical qualitative research that focused on insider experiences has frequently excluded disabled people apart from when the research itself has been about them, or even within other research focused on structural inequalities and marginalized individuals/communities. Many of these critical qualitative research studies have been built upon ableist practices and structures – many of which have implicitly and explicitly focused on "fixing" individual differences. For instance, to date, relatively few scholars have examined how the very methods described as "critical" and in some cases "emancipatory" are exclusionary and serve only *some* audiences. As one example, within qualitative research, the mainstay form of data collection has been interviews. Indeed, this is a taken-for-granted method that typically relies on one speaker (i.e., a researcher) posing a series of questions and most often another speaker (i.e., a research participant) verbally responding to the questions being posed. With advances in technologies, there are now a plethora of ways that interviews can be conducted (e.g., virtually, via chat, etc.; Paulus & Lester, 2022). Nonetheless, what remains the norm is a general reliance of spoken language and conceptualizations of a normative bodymind. Kerschbaum and Price (2017), two disabled scholars, offered an incisive call to center disability, specifically within qualitative interviewing. They noted that even when methodological writing points to ways to conduct interviews in nuanced ways, writers generally foreground "a normative bodymind" (p. 99). Kerchabaum and Price thus argued that the assumptions that undergird much of how qualitative research is designed and carried out are "the result of a persistent lack of attention to disability in research methodologies" (p. 99). There are some exceptions to this claim, and this volume works to build this body of work further.

Organization of the book and overview of the chapters

Beyond this introductory chapter, the book includes six chapters, with Chapter 2 serving to situate and frame the discussion and Chapter 7 designed to offer a call to the qualitative research community. More particularly, in Chapter 2, we (Nusbaum and Lester) engage with Judith Butler's (1993) provocative question, "How, then, might one alter the very terms that constitute the 'necessary' domain of bodies through rendering unthinkable and unlivable another domain of bodies, those that do not matter in the same way" (p. xi)? In thinking with Butler's question, we work to examine how ableist, normative practices in qualitative research function to privilege and center that which is *legible*. In doing so, we call for envisioning and pursuing a qualitative research practice that thinks with bodyminds rendered unthinkable and unlivable. We argue that to "read" disability on the bodymind of a researcher or participant, we become limited by the logic of who we imagine as present in the qualitative research community and what is possible in qualitative inquiry. Grounding this argument is our recognition that critical qualitative research communities should include

> not just the easily assimilated able-disabled but our brothers and sisters who have the most to lose in becoming visible – those who are completely socially marginalized, stigmatized, and hidden away in institutions. . . . What they know, how they know, and why it matters is most threatening to the status quo.
>
> (Sandahl as cited in McRuer & Johnson, 2014, p. 157)

In Chapter 3, Klar and Wolfond write a collaborative chapter that turns inside-out what conceptions of language and expression *are*, and in doing so engage with art, movement, and proprioception to, in Wolfond's words, "relanguage autism." Their piece highlights the public and social demand for "self-same movement and speed" as bodies move throughout the world, and also the horizontal and vertical spatial orientations that guide neurotypical experiences of being and movement. Klar and Wolfond beautifully describe a form of expression that emerges through inextricably linked forms of movement and relational connection, and highlight how this has shaped the creation of an artistic collective of individuals that rely on the process of *disassembly* in the production of art, language, and meaning. Klar and Wolfond's work offers possibilities far outside the normative conceptions of schooling and living for autistic individuals. Their work instead provides a beautiful consideration of care and care networking, guided by relational and affective ways of being, to ameliorate the range of injustices that historically and currently exclude autistic bodies (speaking and nonspeaking) from full participation in society.

Building further, in Chapter 4, Sitter and Grittner write from their experiences as community-based researchers, pointing to their longstanding work applying arts-based media in participatory action research studies with disabled activists. Notably, over the years, this collective work has influenced legislation changes and informed policy around programming and services, while simultaneously raising awareness about the injustices disabled people face. Alongside these implications, Sitter and Grittner pose important methodological questions about group participation in participatory, community work. They wonder what might happen when participation is inaccessible or functions to overwhelm individuals who may desire to participate. They point to barriers that may be built in the environment, making participation and sharing experiences inaccessible. They trouble notions of participation and highlight the potentiality of re-envisioning a more radical conception of participation.

In Chapter 5, Kerschbaum propels the discussion further as she argues for inclusivity in qualitative interview research. With a focus on signing deaf participants and researchers, Kerschbaum powerfully calls for qualitative researchers to engage key challenges around who is positioned as producing knowledge in interview research, sign language transcription, and the work that is required to engage with signed interview interactions. What this chapter highlights is that inclusive qualitative research is not simply about recruiting people from particular groups, but rather involves creating conditions that engage participation.

Illustrating the very notion of inclusive qualitative research, in Chapter 6, Wong, a disabled activist and media maker, traces her journey of using qualitative research methods in creating an online archive and media to foreground disability advocacy, culture, and wisdom. Wong offers an accessible account of her journey in archiving disabled experiencing, highlighting her well-known Disability Visibility Project. We suggest that this chapter serves as a key example of what it might look like when centering disability serves to advance qualitative methods and methodologies.

Finally, in Chapter 7, Pearson and Dickens point to the historical legacy of qualitative research and its contribution as related to disability. They highlight the long history of objectifying disabled bodyminds through exclusion. They offer emancipatory disability research frameworks that encourage collective collaboration with the aim of co-producing inclusive research practices. They engage with critical questions that leave open the possibility for doing qualitative research in radically different ways. We chose to close the volume with this chapter because we believe this chapter points to both the futures of a form of critical qualitative inquiry that centers disability and to the potential challenges of making such a move to center that which has rarely been centered.

Conclusion

We acknowledge that the contributions in this volume are only one step into the shallow edges of an expansive and flowing body of water – a body of water that meanders, rushes, sometimes gets caught and slows, and moves far into the horizon. And yet, we argue, this volume brings together significant and previously unmade arguments that offer the critical, qualitative research community ways to uncover taken-for-granted norms and (re) position an even wider array of bodyminds within our research practices. More specifically, we acknowledge this current moment in time and the demand for knowledge production from disabled, Black, Indigenous, and People of Color, and other multiply marginalized communities within and outside of the academy (c.f. Nusbaum & Lopez, 2020). At the same time, we want to call attention to the inherent tensions that exist when research based in the academy attempts to also ground itself in grassroots knowledge that is generated within local communities. We thus encourage that as you read you foreground disabled, grassroots wisdom and multiply marginalized ways of knowing and of being in the world, and open yourself to futures that speak to the almost endless possibilities of what has not existed previously.

References

Butler, J. (1993). *Bodies that matter: On the discursive limits of sex*. New York: Routledge.

Carspecken, P. F. (1996). *Critical ethnography in educational research: A theoretical and practical guide*. New York: Routledge.

Denzin, N. K. (2017). Critical qualitative inquiry. *Qualitative Inquiry, 23*(1), 8–16.

Denzin, N. K., & Lincoln, Y. S. (Eds.). (2017). *The Sage handbook of qualitative research*. Thousand Oaks, CA: Sage.

Flick, U. (Ed.). (2017). Challenges for a new critical qualitative inquiry. *Qualitative Inquiry, 23*(1), 3–7.

Giroux, H. A. (1982). Culture and rationality in Frankfurt School thought: Ideological foundations for a theory of social education. *Theory & Research in Social Education, 9*(4), 17–55.

Goodley, D. (2013). Dis/entangling critical disability studies. *Disability & Society, 28*(5), 631–644.

Kerschbaum, S., & Price, M. (2017). Centering disability in qualitative interviewing. *Research on the Teaching of English, 52*(1), 98–107.

Kilgore, D. W. (2001). Critical and postmodern perspectives on adult learning. *New Directions for Adult and Continuing Education, 89*, 53–61.

Kinchloe, J., & McLaren, P. (1994). *You can't get to the yellow brick road from here*. New York & London: Routledge.

Lester, J. N., & Nusbaum, E. A. (2018). Reclaiming disability in critical, qualitative research [Special issue]. *Qualitative Inquiry, 24*(1). https://doi.org/10.1177/1077800417727761

Lincoln, Y. S., Lynham, S. A., & Guba, E. G. (2018). Paradigmatic controversies, contradictions, and emerging confluences, revisited. In N. K. Denzin & Y. S. Lincoln (Eds.), *The Sage handbook of qualitative research* (5th ed., pp. 108–150). Thousand Oaks, CA: Sage.

McRuer, R., & Johnson, M. (2014). Proliferating cripistemologies: A virtual round-table. *Journal of Literary & Cultural Disability Studies*, 8(2), 149–170.

Mogendorff, K. (2017). Constructive counter-hegemony. *Disability Studies Quarterly*, 37(3). Retrieved from http://dsq-sds.org/article/view/5971

Noblit, G. W., Flores, S. Y., & Murillo, E. G. (Eds.). (2004). *Postcritical ethnography: Reinscribing critique*. Cresskill, NJ: Hampton Press.

Nusbaum, E. A., & Lopez, E. (2020). Introduction: Disability and peace [Special issue]. *Peace Review: A Journal of Social Justice*, 31(4), 433–438. https://doi.org/10.1080/10402659.2019.1800927

Paulus, T. M., & Lester, J. N. (2022). *Doing qualitative research in a digital world*. Thousand Oaks, CA: Sage.

Price, M. (2014). The bodymind problem and the possibilities of pain. *Hypatia*, 30(1), 268–284.

Thomas, J. (1993). *Doing critical ethnography* (Vol. 26). Newbury Park, CA: Sage.

Ulmer, J. B. (2020). Pivots and pirouettes: Carefully turning traditions. *Qualitative Inquiry*, 26(5), 454–457.

2 Bodymind legibility and possibilities for qualitative research

Emily A. Nusbaum and Jessica Nina Lester

Bodymind[1] (Price, 2014) differences have been written about across time and place, with a hypervigilance on and even discomfort with difference being persistently part of society. French theorist Henri-Jacques Stiker (1999) argued that disability can be understood as transhistorically disturbing, as it makes visible that "an aberrancy within the corporeal order is an aberrancy in the social order" (p. 40). Disabled people, he argued, are often oriented to as an ontological threat; that is, they "are the tear in our being" (p. 10). Indeed, even the oldest historical documents included descriptions of physical and psychological differences (Braddock & Parish, 2001), with an emphasis on bodies framed as *illegible* (Butler, 1993). Such bodyminds are those that are often imagined as being "unthinkable, abject, unlivable" (Butler, p. x), and we suggest are often "completely socially marginalized, stigmatized, and hidden away in institutions" (Sandahl as cited in McRuer & Johnson, 2014, p. 157). We argue that this understanding of *illegible* bodyminds has long pervaded much of social life, including academic fields and scholarly writing. In many ways, the privileging of *legible* bodyminds has become a taken-for-granted practice and part of the Norm. As Foucault (1995) wrote, "the power of the Norm appears through the disciplines. . . . Let us say rather that, since the eighteenth century, it has joined other powers – the Law, the Word (*Parole*) and the Text, Tradition – imposing new delimitations upon them" (p. 184).

In this chapter, we work to foreground what it might mean for critical qualitative researchers to center disability and begin to imagine bodyminds that have long been excluded from methodological discussions and the very development of methods. To do so, we think with a question posed by Butler (1993) in *Bodies that Matter:* "How, then, might one alter the very terms that constitute the 'necessary' domain of bodies through rendering unthinkable and unlivable another domain of bodies, those that do not matter in the same way" (p. xi)? We engage with this question and Butler's writing around *illegible* bodies in an effort to examine the ways in which ableist, normative practices in qualitative research function to privilege and center that which is *legible*. In doing so, we call for envisioning and pursuing a qualitative research practice that thinks with bodyminds rendered unthinkable and unlivable. We do this while offering two cautionary reminders to readers. First, we agree with the assessment that applications of Butler's theories to disability should occur with care and critique (see, Samuels, 2002, for a deeper discussion of this point). Indeed, Butler never wrote the word "disability" or "disabled bodies" in *Bodies that Matter*; yet this is the writing of Butler that has been argued to be "the most easily adapted to the subjects and goals of disability studies" (Samuels, p. 59). More particularly, Samuels cautioned:

> because much of Butler's work appears highly applicable to disability, one is certainly tempted to draw upon her important critical insights while exchanging the term disability for the original term of sex/ gender. However, I would like to suggest the need for rigorous critical scrutiny of the implications of such an exchange. In its most extreme forms, this exchange can become an apparent substitution that suggests a direct correspondence or equation between two very different realms of social and bodily existence.
>
> (p. 64)

We concur and yet still find it productive and generative to engage with the question that Butler posed. Nonetheless, we ourselves – and we hope readers as well – engage the ideas we present here with a measure of critique and caution. Second, this is a notably abbreviated discussion of very layered concepts and ideas. Thus, what we offer in the next few pages is meant to serve as the start of a conversation about how Butler's question might provoke and expand the work of qualitative researchers.

Considering Butler's question we also center Kafer's (2013) discussion regarding the need for disability to be *legibly* read on the body – a discussion which has implications for the ways in which qualitative research and researchers have responded to considering disability/disabled participants through accommodation and/or protecting a population deemed "vulnerable." Thus, with this mandate to "read" disability on the bodymind of a researcher or participant, we become limited, we argue, by the logic of who we imagine as present in the qualitative research community and what is possible in qualitative inquiry. To engage this further, we structure our discussion around four primary questions:

1   What are illegible bodyminds?
2   How does engaging with cripistemologies shape our understanding about bodyminds and the qualitative research process more generally?

3   How might Butler's (1993) question generate new practices and ways
      of being for the qualitative research community?

4   What are the pragmatic implications of engaging with bodyminds pre-
      viously rendered "unthinkable" and "unlivable"?

(Butler, 1993, p. xi)

By engaging with these questions, we aim to invite a generative dialogue
around the implications for the qualitative research community, specifically
as we continue to grapple with the implications of centering disability (Lester & Nusbaum, 2018).

What are il/legible bodies/minds?

In considering Butler's question, we place the assertion of Kuntz (2016) at
the forefront – that there is a need within qualitative work for:

> an articulated vision for alternative spaces of possibility, places where
> we might act and be as other than we currently are . . . often such spaces
> of possibility extend from the recognition that previously legitimated
> forms of knowing and being (epistemological and ontological assump-
> tions, respectively) misrepresent others' lived realities.

(p. 14)

And we argue that our efforts to examine the ways in which ableist, normative practices in qualitative research function to privilege and center that
which is *legible* must consider these spaces of possibility. Previous work
(Nusbaum & Lester, 2019) has posited that one of these "alternative spaces
of possibility" involves "crip horizons" – horizons that engage the alternative possibility in which disability is "rendered desirable, and the structures
which surround it, profoundly contested" (Kolářová, 2014, p. 257), while
at the same time acknowledging that "'cripness' is an impossible location;
it is unintelligible and lies beyond the conceivable, thinkable, and imagin-
able (political) horizon" (p. 259). Thus, when we even consider thinking
with Butler's (1993) question – "How, then, might one alter the very terms
that constitute the 'necessary' domain of bodies through rendering unthinkable and unlivable another domain of bodies, those that do not matter in
the same way?" (p. xi) – we are required to engage with those bodyminds
often deemed transhistorically disturbing. For critical qualitative researchers working within/towards "crip horizons" it becomes necessary to engage
with the many bodyminds that *most people do not even know exist* (Meekosha, 1998; *our emphasis*) in ways that move beyond simply accommodations, as is the typical response.

An additional component of this working towards "crip horizons" in critical qualitative inquiry is to acknowledge our own (unconscious) privileging of a concept described by Garland-Thomson (1997) as "the normate" – or the composite identity status held by those who are not stigmatized by identifiers of disability (or other devalued identities). Thus, in qualitative research communities, the legible bodymind is "the normate," although this only becomes clear in the design, implementation, analysis, and distribution of qualitative research when, as Garland-Thomson indicated, "we scrutinize the social processes and discourses that constitute physical and cultural otherness" (p. 8). The assumption – or even imagination – of who is in our research communities and spaces becomes limited through the tacit acceptance of "the normate" – of bodyminds that are legible – and through this acceptance we fail to acknowledge this truth: "What they know, how they know, and why it matters is most threatening to the status quo" (Sandahl, as cited by McRuer & Johnson, 2014, p. 157). Finally, working at the edges of "crip horizons" allows us to re-envision all that we name critical qualitative inquiry, as we work to locate disabled people at the center of knowledge production (McRuer & Johnson, 2014).

How does engaging with cripistemologies shape our understanding about bodies/minds and the qualitative research process more generally?

Minich (2016, 2017) asserted the primacy of disability and disability studies, not as a field of study, but rather as a methodology, noting methodological concern about the separation of the study of marginalized locations and those who occupy them, as they relate to disability. Minich's work is advanced further by Hickman and Serlin (2018), who ask "how might scholars develop methodological tools that are not only specific to critical disability studies, but also anchor and apply perceptual, sensorial, and experiential dimensions of what it means to be a disabled subject in the first place?" (p. 155). Hickman and Serlin added the important caveat, related to the subjectivity of the disabled bodymind: "how might we begin to situate our crip subjectivities, especially when, like all subjectivities, they are fluid and in a perpetual state of becoming . . . how might we embody both our knowledge and our methods?" (p. 155). This is a useful question to consider as we advance our own body of work – to move cripistemology beyond its status as a neologism, and position it instead as a valued and necessary way of knowing that can shape and advance practices in qualitative inquiry beyond the status quo. That is, "particularly because of the decision to be unstable, incapable, unwilling, disabled (the sharpness of this 'cannot') opens up a world of possibility" (Johnson & McRuer, p. 137) and offers a potential bridge to considering the ways in which disability pushes back on the demand for bodymind legibility within qualitative inquiry. This informs and supports our work here as we think with Butler and what her work affords our arguments within and across our own emerging body of work.

In our previous consideration of cripistemology within critical qualitative inquiry for the social sciences (Nusbaum & Lester, 2019), we have attempted "to attend to rejected and extraordinary bodies, and at the same time to explore disability at the places where bodily edges and categorical distinctions blur or dissolve (where the disabled body as literal referent is, if not dematerialized, then differently materialized)" (Johnson & McRuer, 2014, p. 132). As an example of the latter, we turn to Jasbir K. Puar, whose work renders the concept of disability knowledge unstable in useful ways for our own thinking with Butler here. Johnson and McRuer referenced Puar (2011), noting "her concern with 'precarious populations' both destabilizes the category of disability and opens its borders" (p. 135) – or perhaps for our argument here – its horizons to include more and different kinds of bodily and affective experiences. Johnson and McRuer's reference to Puar in their discussion of the emergence of cripistemologies reminds us that inclusion necessarily relies on exclusion, which addresses our desire to turn inside out (Lester & Nusbaum, 2018) previous scholarship around disability and methodology represented in work such as Berger and Lorenz (2015), who contended that there are few disability-specific research methods courses in institutions of higher education. Instead, we position cripistemologies – in all that it could encompass, generate, and provide – as a methodological movement to destabilize traditional ways of knowing about disability as they are reinforced in normative (ableist) ways of considering disability within qualitative inquiry in the social sciences.

Johnson and McRuer also articulated the "tendencies towards instability" that cripistemologies necessarily invoke (p. 133). We find this describes well the open-ended and almost unanswerable questions that we previously offered (Nusbaum & Lester, 2019). Specifically, we asked in what ways can cripistemologies challenge us to:

- Identify what identities come into play as we center and entangle disability?
- Consider insider/outsider statuses differently? How and why do we move between these locations, and how does this allow us to push back on these and other distinct binaries?
- Understand what "counts" as embodied experience and expose what is left in/out of text when we use normative narrative strategies to describe embodiment?

- Articulate the ways in which critical qualitative inquiry might become a co-performance between researcher and research participants?
- Work to move identity beyond stating positionality – and instead consider relationality?
- Advance notions of reflexivity and understand research and research practice as historical, contextual, and material?

Finally, we must remember and even prioritize, as both Meekosha (1998) and Sandahl (as cited in McRuer & Johnson, 2014) remind us, cripistemologies must include all possible bodyminds, and especially those with whom we cannot imagine dissolving the self/other divide.

How might Butler's question generate new practices and ways of being for the qualitative research community?

At its core, to think with Butler's (1993) question – "How, then, might one alter the very terms that constitute the 'necessary' domain of bodies through rendering unthinkable and unlivable another domain of bodies, those that do not matter in the same way" (p. xi) – invites the qualitative research community to critically evaluate *who* typically participates as a researcher and/or research participant, *how* we write (or even do not write) about participants and bodyminds, and *what* qualitative methods and methodologies make visible about the bodyminds that are privileged (most often in implicit ways). When considering Butler's (1993) discussion of body legibility, we can push the boundaries – that is, the horizons – of these questions further, as we recognize the ways that the demand for legibility privileges a bodymind that can be read or understood in normative, taken-for-granted ways. Mandated legibility is coupled with the devalued, if not fully erased, ontology of disability (Nusbaum & Steinborn, 2019) – and in so doing, ableist epistemologies are taken up as truth. It is imperative then – as Butler's question propels us – to accept that this demand for legibility is not a neutral demand, especially when considering devalued bodies. As Ho, Kerschbaum, Sanchez, and Yergeau (2020) noted, "Neutrality, like normalcy, can operate at the level of assumptions about who gets to exist in certain spaces" (p. 127). While Ho et al. wrote about their experiences as disabled academic-teachers, we believe their arguments apply to a research context as well. As they noted, their very "presence needs to be explained and defended over, and over, and over, and over again as worthy" (p. 127). Indeed, "ideologies are written through disability on *bodyminds*" (p. 127) and when disabled bodyminds live and move through neutral systems, they "are further marginalized when we cannot – or do not – enact neutrality" (p. 127).

So, then, where might we see this emerge within qualitative research practice? We believe there are many examples of this and point to one here. Kerschbaum and Price (2017) wrote of how interview methods – a mainstay and privileged qualitative approach – center a normative body-mind. They illustrated how centering disability and varied forms of embodied experience has implications for qualitative interviewing research design, writing:

> Centering disability is about much more than simply compensating for or including disabled researchers and participants. Rather, it means posing the question: If we assume that disability is part of the qualitative interview situation, how does that unsettle commonplace assumptions about qualitative interviewing?
>
> (p. 98)

The authors highlighted how even within methods texts that discuss interviewing practices, "a normative interview context" is assumed where the interview is assumed to "proceed aurally/orally" (p. 99). They further noted that:

> Another assumption is that interviewers are hyper-able research instruments capable of flexing and bending to any circumstance or situation they might encounter in their work. The importance of accommodating participating is often emphasized, without mention of the fact that the interviewer might need to accommodate herself as well.
>
> (p. 99)

Interviews, like so many qualitative methods, are built around bodyminds that are rendered *thinkable* and *livable*. We suggest that to imagine otherwise troubles historical understandings of what it means to be a researcher or research participant and leaves open the possibility to question the very basis of how research is conceptualized and conducted. Yet, this is what we believe thinking with Butler's question provokes.

To build this argument further, we carried out a brief review of the qualitative methodological literature that speaks to concerns related to disability. First, we searched for all relevant articles within the literature, using various derivations of the following search terms: "qualitative research," "disability," "disabled," and "disability studies." Second, we conducted searches in key qualitative methodology journals, such as *Qualitative Inquiry, Qualitative Research*, the *International Journal of Qualitative Studies in Education*, among others. Third, we reviewed all abstracts, selecting only those articles that explicitly discussed disability and the qualitative research process. Further, in our review, we gave particular attention to those qualitative writings that seek to teach qualitative research practices and introduce theories of being-knowing. Ultimately, we located 19 methodological articles that explicitly engaged with notions of disability as related to engaging/participating in qualitative research. Significantly, our review examined how disabled people were positioned and the extent to which disability was foregrounded/ backgrounded. We noted three general patterns across the literature. First, some authors produced methods-focused discussions, wherein the impacts of disabled people on the process of conducting qualitative research were centered. That is, in these particular articles, the authors centered their practices (e.g., conducting an interview) and emphasized how they were challenged to adapt their practice. Second, some authors called for participatory methodologies and practices as the means by which to engage in inclusive research. These particular articles emphasized how disabled voices might be foregrounded and positioned as central within the qualitative research process. Third, some of the methodological literature critiqued normative qualitative research, foregrounding the problems common to qualitative research practice broadly.

This unsettling of "commonplace assumptions," while less common in the methodological literature, did appear to be a relatively recent and growing trend.

What is significant about these general patterns is the focus on implications for data collection and general calls for participatory methodological approaches, with relatively few examinations of the ways in which ableist, normative expectations might be interrogated. Here is where we continue to push against the work of Berger and Lorenz (2015), who focused on methods-related issues associated with specific impairments and the need for researcher reflexivity – and, as we previously asserted (Lester & Nusbaum, 2018), we work, instead, "to create a space in which disability advances the use of critical qualitative methods and methodologies to more specifically attend to and develop new meanings about disability" (p. 2). For us, Butler's question leads us to work to create spaces wherein disability advances methods and methodologies and we begin to think with "unthinkable" and presumably "unlivable" bodyminds.

What are the pragmatic implications of engaging with bodyminds previously rendered "unthinkable" and "unlivable"?

Writing to the qualitative research community, Denzin (2017) noted that "this is a historical present that cries out for emancipatory visions, for visions that inspire transformative inquiries, and for inquiries that can provide the moral authority to move people to struggle and resist oppression" (p. 8). We suggest that *centering* disability and *engaging* with bodyminds that have long been positioned – implicitly and explicitly – to be unthinkable and unlivable is one way that we might respond to Denzin's call. This, we argue, is an "emancipatory vision" that actively works against the hegemonic power of ableism and ableist epistemologies that have for so long been minimally discussed and rarely acknowledged within the methodological community. Indeed, as we have argued elsewhere (Lester & Nusbaum, 2018), even critically oriented qualitative scholarship has served to perpetuate ableistic agendas and assumptions about being and knowing. Notably, ableism can be understood as a set of state sanctioned processes and practices whereby socio-cultural misconceptions of disability, as well as negative attitudes and behaviors toward disabled people in the everyday, result in institutionalized oppression. Hunt (1966) wrote, "Disabled people 'are set apart from the ordinary' in ways which see them as they pose a direct 'challenge' to commonly held social values by appearing 'unfortunate, useless, different, oppressed and sick'" (p. 146). Institutionalized biases thus represent a systematic obstacle to disabled peoples' equal access to social services, healthcare, transportation, education, independent living, community participation, self-determination, self-direction, marriage, child rearing, and so on. These biases manifest themselves at the interpersonal, cultural, and institutional levels, thus pushing disabled experiences into cultural silos and disabled bodies into social and economic precarity and even death (Acevedo Espinal, 2018, p. 1).

So, for qualitative researchers to take up Butler's question means that we commit to advancing qualitative methods and methodological discussions from the ways in which "disabled people" are viewed primarily as "research informants who have little say about the intellectual purposes their input serves which may lead to underuse of disabled people's experiential expertise" (Mogendorff, 2017, p. np), to a place where disability embodiment and the lived experience of disability are potential sources of method and methodological advancement. In many ways, this kind of work has already begun. For example, in a 2018 special issue of *Qualitative Inquiry* six authors "reclaimed" disability in a variety of critical ways – ranging from post-structuralist/new materialist approaches (De Schauwer, Van De Putte, & Davies, 2018), to specific methods offerings (Annamma, 2018; Castrodale, 2018; Shankar, 2018), as well as methodological critiques of concepts such as identity, positionality, reflexivity, similitude, and voice (Chaudhry, 2018; Teachman, McDonough, Macarthur, & Gibson, 2018). As another example, the process of centering disability (Kershbaum & Price, 2017) was reflected in a recent conference roundtable (Nusbaum et al., 2018) that examined methodological challenges related to normative and ableist assumptions of doing qualitative research. The range of papers included in this roundtable demonstrated that there is no singular answer to questions about method and methodology – but rather the centering of diverse bodyminds complicates the normative desire to create methods and methodologies that are 'standard,' versus thinking about methods and methodologies as fluid, emerging, and disruptive – as the disabled bodymind requires.

Importantly, a central implication of engaging with bodyminds previously rendered unthinkable and unlivable is that the qualitative research community commits to include:

> not just the easily assimilated able-disabled but our brothers and sisters who have the most to lose in becoming visible – those who are completely socially marginalized, stigmatized, and hidden away in institutions. . . . What they know, how they know, and why it matters is most threatening to the status quo.
>
> (Sandahl as cited in McRuer & Johnson, 2014, p. 157)

Doing so, we suggest, can lead to re-envisioning the very methods that we have long used to study and examine people's lives and everyday experiences, and expand *who* participates in and even leads research. Methodology is always becoming and what we suggest Butler's question provokes is new possibilities and visions for how we *do* qualitative research and *be* qualitative researchers.

Conclusions

To conclude, we invite the qualitative research community, and qualitative researchers specifically, to not only sit with Butler's question, but also consider the following four questions related to the design and implementation of qualitative research studies. As to be expected, these are not questions with singular or static answers. Rather, they are questions for researchers and students of qualitative research alike to grapple with in considering how to authentically and purposefully center diverse bodyminds in critical qualitative inquiry:

1 Where are the places/spaces that the qualitative research community can grapple with questions about designing qualitative research that centers disabled bodyminds as critical, intersectional, and necessary when pursuing socially just and potentially emancipatory research?
2 What are methods-focused considerations related to data-collection practices (such as observation, interviews, or fieldnote documentation) that need to be re-thought and re-conceived of as we both *assume* and *invite* participation, creation, and research designs from bodyminds previously unseen?
3 What are the research practices that qualitative researchers can engage in as they work to undo previously unexamined (and ableist) considerations about what 'counts' as research design, implementation, and analysis?

4   What are specific actions that qualitative researchers can take to challenge, stretch, and bend the confines of what has historically been positioned as "rigorous" qualitative inquiry in the social sciences?

Note

1   "Bodymind" is a term that was first used by Margaret Price (2014) and serves to make explicit how the body and the mind are always already intertwined.

References

Acevedo Espinal, S. (2018). *Enabling geographies: Neurodivergence, self-authorship, and the politics of social space* [Doctoral dissertation]. California Institute of Integral Studies. ProQuest Dissertations & Theses Global, Publication No. 10815948.

Annamma, S. A. (2018). Mapping consequential geographies in the carceral state: Education journey mapping as a qualitative method with girls of color with dis/abilities. *Qualitative Inquiry, 24*(1), 20–34.

Berger, R. J., & Lorenz, L. (2015). *Disability and qualitative inquiry: Methods for rethinking an ableist world.* Boston, MA: Ashgate Publishers.

Braddock, D. L., & Parish, S. L. (2001). An institutional history of disability. In G. L. Albrecht, K. D. Seelman, & M. Bury (Eds.), *Handbook of disability studies* (pp. 11–68). Thousand Oaks, CA: Sage.

Butler, J. (1993). *Bodies that matter: On the discursive limits of sex.* New York: Routledge.

Castrodale, M. A. (2018). Mobilizing dis/ability research: A critical discussion of qualitative go-along interviews in practice. *Qualitative inquiry, 24*(1), 45–55.

Chaudhry, V. (2018). Knowing through tripping: A performative praxis for co-constructing knowledge as a disabled halfie. *Qualitative Inquiry, 24*(1), 70–82.

Denzin, N. K. (2017). Critical qualitative inquiry. *Qualitative Inquiry, 23*(1), 8–16.

De Schauwer, E., Van De Putte, I., & Davies, B. (2018). Collective biography: Using memory work to explore the space-in-between normativity and difference/disability. *Qualitative Inquiry, 24*(1), 8–19.

Foucault, M. (1995). *Discipline and punish: The birth of the prison.* New York: Vintage.

Garland-Thomson, R. (1997). *Extraordinary bodies: Figuring physical disability in American culture and literature.* New York: Columbia University Press.

Hickman, L., & Serlin, D. (2018). Towards a crip methodology for critical disability studies. In K. Ellis, R. Garland-Thomson, M. Kent, & R. Robertson (Eds.), *Interdisciplinary approaches to disability: Looking towards the future* (Vol. 2, pp. 131–141). New York: Routledge.

Ho, A. B. T., Kerschbaum, S. L., Sanchez, R., & Yergeau, M. (2020). Cripping Neutrality: Student Resistance, Pedagogical Audiences, and Teachers' Accommodations. *Pedagogy: Critical Approaches to Teaching Literature, Language, Composition, and Culture, 20*(1), 127–139.

Hunt, P. (1966). A critical condition. In P. Hunt (Ed.), *Stigma: The experience of disability.* London: Geoffrey Chapman.

Kafer, A. (2013). *Feminist, queer, crip.* Bloomington, IN: Indiana University Press.

Kerschbaum, S., & Price, M. (2017). Centering disability in qualitative interviewing. *Research on the Teaching of English, 52*(1), 98–107.

Kolářová, K. (2014). The inarticulate post-socialist crip: On the cruel optimism of Neoliberal transformations in the Czech Republic. *Journal of Literary and Cultural Disability Studies,* 8(3), 257–274.

Kuntz, A. M. (2016). *The responsible methodologist: Inquiry, truth-telling, and social justice.* Routledge.

Lester, J. N., & Nusbaum, E. A. (Eds.). (2018). "Reclaiming" disability in critical qualitative research. *Qualitative Inquiry, 24*(1).

McRuer, R., & Johnson, M. (2014). Proliferating cripistemologies: A virtual roundtable. *Journal of Literary & Cultural Disability Studies,* 8(2), 149–170.

Meekosha, H. (1998). Body battles: Bodies, gender and disability. In T. Shakespeare (Ed.), *The disability reader: Social science perspectives* (pp. 163–180). London: Cassell.

Minich, J. A. (2016). Enabling whom? Critical disability studies now. *Lateral: Journal of the Cultural Studies Association, 5*(1). Retrieved from https://csalateral. org/issue/5-1/forum-alt-humanities-critical-disability-studies-now-minich/

Minich, J. A. (2017). Thinking with Jina B. Kim and Sami Schalk. *Lateral: Journal of the Cultural Studies Association, 5*(1). Retrieved from https://csalateral.org/ issue/6-1/forum-alt-humanities-critical-disability-studies-response-minich/

Mogendorff, K. (2017). Constructive counter-hegemony. *Disability Studies Quarterly, 37*(3). Retrieved from http://dsq-sds.org/article/view/5971

Nusbaum, E. A., Lester, J. N., Dickens, B., Valente, J., Chaudry, V., & Schauwver, E. (2018). Centering disability in critical qualitative research. *Roundtable presented at the American Education Research Association annual conference,* New York, NY.

Nusbaum, E. A., & Lester, J. N. (2019, April). From the center to the horizon: Engaging "crip horizons" in critical qualitative inquiry. *American Educational Research Association.* Toronto, Canada.

Nusbaum, E. A., & Steinborn, M. (2019). Ontological erasure: New possibilities for "visibilizing" disability studies in curriculum [Special issue]. *Journal of Curriculum Theorizing, 43*(1), 24–35. Retrieved from https://journal.jctonline.org/index. php/jct/article/view/764/385

Price, M. (2014). The bodymind problem and the possibilities of pain. *Hypatia, 30*(1), 268–284.

Puar, J. K. (2011). The cost of getting better: Suicide, sensation, switchpoints. *GLA: A Journal of Lesbian and Gay Studies, 18*(1), 149–158.

Samuels, E. (2002). Critical divides: Judith Butler's body theory and the question of disability. *NWSA journal,* 58–76.

Shankar, S. (2018). An autoethnography about recovering awareness following brain injury: Is my truth valid? *Qualitative Inquiry, 24*(1), 56–69.

Stiker, H. J. (1999). *A history of disability.* Ann Arbor, MI: University of Michigan Press.

Teachman, G., McDonough, P., Macarthur, C., & Gibson, B. E. (2018). A critical dialogical methodology for conducting research with disabled youth who use augmentative and alternative communication. *Qualitative Inquiry, 24*(1), 35–44.

3 Neurodiversity in relation

Artistic intraethnographic practice

Estée Klar and Adam Wolfond

"I am the pace of my body and not language" – Adam Wolfond
(2019, p. 2)

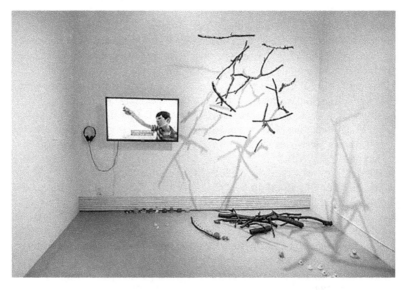

Figure 3.1 Exhibition film installation, S/Pace was part of the *Access is Love and Love is Complicated* Exhibit, October–December 2019 at Critical Distance Centre for Curators, Toronto. This piece emerged from several years of experimentation with poetry, sticks and movement. In one segment of the film, Adam Wolfond who is non-speaking and uses a text-to-speech device, writes of a neurodivergent world he would build: "I would build architecture other than the open space in a world that would then have gravity to be settled. I would basically design a world of water where we could sometimes be about swimming and the water pressure would help to feel the body. The rubber toys would be everywhere and the sticks would always be in range of reach." He has now extended into a process where he is thinking about "the neurodivergent city that is already here" (forthcoming). The installation film can be viewed at esteerelation.com.

Intraethnography and neurodiversity as relation

"Art is the open way of telling," writes my non-speaking autistic son and collaborator, Adam Wolfond, who types to express himself in words. His lexicon is full of *open* and *all ways*, gesturing not towards a narrative that's separated from the moment of its coming into being (and therefore as afterthought enacted in the process of editing), but rather, an open way of "languaging" experience (Wolfond), wayfaring in movement, bringing back into the foreground what is perceived and felt immediately – otherwise backgrounded in most narrative and academic forms. Being open might seem paradoxical to "needing gravity to be settled," but as always in his work, the paradox dances: "Open is how I think/Open is how I feel/Open is like water/Water forges toward the long way of thought/the way the water always/moves is like the way I think/toward movement" (Wolfond, 2019, p. 4). The need for being open *and* feeling settled is a perpetual flying-landing (Adam's description) movement. "I need good support to land my thoughts on the keyboard" (Wolfond, conversation). My presence, a light touch on his back, helps Adam to write, like the "land that buttresses the open water," (Wolfond), to feel settled enough to type, but I am not the only support he uses as he also attunes to the nonhuman. As Erin Manning, Remi Yergeau and others remind us, many autistics cannot subtract the detail of the environment; unable to filter it to move or speak the way neurotypicals do. "Like water I always move" (ibid, 1); water suggests immersion. In his face all the time, there are objects and affective calls that lure right now. "Needing gravity to be settled," as he says in the film installation, Adam rethinks the nature of support – human and nonhuman – in a world where neurotypicality moves too quickly, with rules for movement, often ignoring these affective calls and feels that Adam cannot ignore. Adam summons support for the neurodiverse ways in our artistic practice. In his own words, the open way, he "relanguages autism."

In our artistic-movement practice we *attune* to the *ecological milieu*,[1] drawing on affect theory, thinking also of other art theories such as *happenings*, although unlike the work of Allan Kaprow and the 1950s, we don't seek to be performative or scripted. When attuning to the ecological milieu, we move within it, noticing modes of expression emerging in what Adam calls "languaging," as well as in/corporeal[2] "patterning" and "arranging," reminding that bodymindworld are interconnected. Expression is an intrarelational bodying, worlding *and* languaging – all tethered, entangled and weaving together, unable to excise experience from the moment of occurrence that Adam refers to as pacing and rallying. Brian Massumi and Erin Manning have named this *immediation*: "autistic experience or autistic mode of perception has a lot in common with that emergent level of immediation"[3] (Massumi, 2015, p. 128). As a mode of perception, Adam and I think of how proprioception-synesthesia-movement co-operate in a "visual" field that is "scattered," as he blurs the field with a "twallowing" (his word) stick to "see" and move.[4] "Seeing", after all is about feeling and touching. And yet another paradox emerges: "I am able to scatter/and I move with the colors around me like a good/questioning dance/I am able to scatter/the man of autism is rallying/the colors of life to move" (Wolfond, 2019, p. 41). To scatter is also an *ability and a mode of perception*, a way of moving with affects and objects to move. Simply put, proprioception can be described as spacing space, and synesthesia, a merging of sensory perception (as in tasting color) and we are suggesting that these phenomena cannot be separated. Movement is required for Adam to see and move through the "scattered" world, as he describes in a multitude of ways how he blurs the field to make it whole. Movement through – from one point to the next – can be a perilous experience that Adam manages by tapping rubber bath toys to create or keep the pace, waving sticks in front of his eyes, or following another body closely.

In her speculative piece on perception and movement, *Helen Keller or Arakawa* (1994), Madeline Gins writes:

> How do I move? I can only move by eating up and dissolving where I am. I (anyone) pull in with a bright gulp what is to come next. When walking forward, I also snake along three parallel, horizontal planes. I case standpoints and send out runners or tendrils of what I call forming spacetime.
>
> (1994, p. 11)

Proprioception-synesthesia-movement is how Adam keeps aligning-spacing-timing as it were – a take on Adam's "I line my pace" with sticks, with other bodies because the transition (that is perceived as being in the midst), so busy, is experienced all at once whereas many of us don't have to think so hard about moving from point to point. We are able to subtract this excess. "Grasping toward through" (Manning, 2020, p. 17) is the way of aligning – the way of bodying, worlding, feeling and languaging at once, in transition; pace, rhythm, weight – patterns arrange the ways. It's not easy. It can be downright anxiety-provoking, particularly when others expect self-same movement and speed. "Really way of touching the world is/the way I am wanting/with my tics" (Wolfond, 2019, p. 30). A tic or a hesitation, typically ascribed to Tourettes syndrome or tic "disorder",[5] is "eating up and dissolving where I am," preparing for the next move. "Ticcing through the world is like touching it." A tic, or a stim,[6] is also *grasping toward through*; it is motional-relational that involves this mode of perception and expression. Brian Massumi writes, proprioception is "movement-vision turned proprioceptive" (in Savarese, 2012). We can't think of vision as separated from other forms of sensing or what we refer to support as touching-feeling, or affective: "Synesthetic forms are dynamic," writes Massumi, "They are not mirrored in thought; they are literal perceptions. . . . Synesthetic forms are used by being summoned into present perception then recombined with an experience of movement. And they are useful. They serve as memory aides and orientation devices" (Massumi, 2002, p. 186). Synesthetes bring forth movement-vision and associative experience into language, slanting (Adam's word) orientation, "pattering" (Adam's word) rubber bath toys to pace, feel, arrange space. He does not speak specifically of the vertical-horizontal to which we typically orient, but towards an objectile field (Manning & Massumi, 2014) of multiple fractalized perceptions and movements – think dendrites and the rhizome. In this sense, I have come to think with Adam about autistic perception as additive and relationally mobile so we have to attune to the *atmospheres* of movement within the ecological milieu – and what collects *en route*. New shapes and forms in relation, expression, writing, art, research . . . merge as we perpetually snake tendrils along. We posit, then, that neurodiversity *is* always in relation on the move.[7] This way of connection and relation rethinks the way of support and care and the problem of inclusion as an appendage to ableist, or what we call neurotypical, "architectures" that Adam describes as too "still."[8]

For many people with disabilities, supports are more visible especially when someone like Adam requires a communication partner, although we suggest that support – that is more than human, more than individual – is utilized by everyone even if it remains unacknowledged as support.[9] We are not individual but becoming in individuation; not a division of bodies, but a morphogenetic becoming. The importance of asynchrony is difference becoming together. It is a way of rethinking ecological mutualism, or what we sometimes refer to as the ecological body – the *intrarelational* body. "Intra," writes Karen Barad,

> is not just a kind of neologism which gets us from interaction, where we start with separate entities and they interact, to intra-action, where there are interactions through which a subject and object emerge, but actually [a] new understanding of causality itself . . . about the possibilities of mutual response.
>
> (Barad, in Dolphijn & Van der Tuin, 2012, p. 55)

We don't often see or even know the cause of what moves us – this *affect* that mutually responds – but we can *feel* it. Artistic work enables us to understand beyond clinical description and fixity as we feel relation and connection in the moving. We can also feel when something is assembling in our movement-artistic practices together. We can question "independent" subjectivity, identity and roles in the collaboration. Adam also gestures towards the multiplicity of affects that de/activate movement,[10] understanding that hesitation and ticcing are also movements in the process of moving which is important in understanding relation and support.

Erin Manning writes, "[o]ther ways of perceiving create other ways of knowing" (2020, p. 27). We ask what constitutes knowledge and research if autistics are merely objects of research by non-autistic researchers. The arts enables us to bring forth new possible *ways* that engage and immerse relationally.[11] The way of support and collaboration thinks about the conditions and techniques that support neurodiversity and shifts the way we think about research as a collaborative process rather than seeking a method or stating a goal about how we think relation and collaboration ought to occur. Conditions reveal themselves in the way our bodies move; techniques emerge when we move together in relation, without a forced directive about how we should move. I came to this realization of how collaboration must become visible in our work when supporting Adam's communication with my hand on his back to help activate his, rhythmic movement to the keyboard,[12] and in understanding the ecological/incorporeal calls he was answering in the environment – feeling with him the affective calls nuances of movement outside the humanist and clinical frames. We named this open "method" – or better put, *way* – *artistic intraethnography* to extend the *inter* that suggests the human duo because there is also the more than human in relation. We *dis assemble* our collective artistic work[13] to not only rethink autism, movement and the way relation is always shifting and never fixed, but also to resist charity and state-run care models that aim to ameliorate autistic traits and segregate autistic people. Dis assembling the ways we collaborate allows for more movement. It resists enforcing a methodology for it. So we can't prescribe fixed methods, but we can explore relation through movement and autistic languaging.[14] Our aim is to never become an "arts program" to rehabilitate autistics but to continue to let our arts collective perpetually dis assemble itself, again avoiding fixity, playing with the creative synergies of relation and becoming. As is autistic experience and expression, we utilize artistic relational processes where we can feel difference emerging rather than attempting to change our *ways*, and again, parse our roles to explain autistic experience, my experience and how we do things. If an explanation arises, be prepared for it to dis assemble into many more expressions, as Adam never provides one answer or cause to a movement or experience.

Bodying worlding walking languaging

Wet

I want to think about ball and the water to water the talking that unravels like wet yarn in saturation of lines rallying the way open directions do and the rally is more than the good people talking but the amazing expansion exiting the word meaning to be languaging that is autistic feeling like ways of water and I want you to want the way I wet the words. I wet words the open way. Open the words not to synthesize the water easy but think

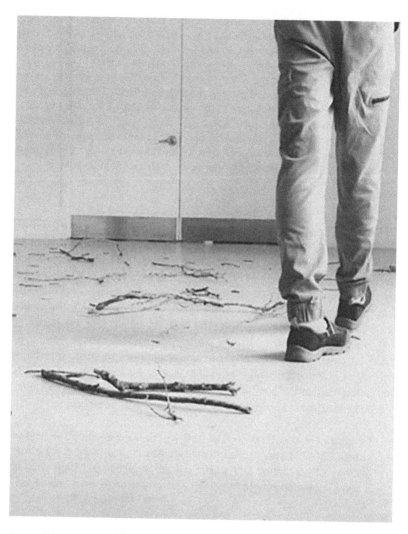

Figure 3.2 Adam dis assembling sticks with movement in studio, 2017.

about the ways water and the world moves to think about bathing the synesthetic experience to walking waters of the words calligraphy ways with
questions about what words about experience mean. I am thinking about
the way people describe synesthesia and opening the ideas about using the
word towards the waters of thought and feeling that want more than words
to describe them. I water the master's language to want more. The master's language wants laps around words that make seeing simple and I want

waters of expression to answer eagerly and toward the way arts want worn experience rallying easy earnest questions to arrange autistic essay of easy fast understanding emanations of the waters. I am rallying a conversation about the salty words that art and literature talks about experience and I want the people to understand pace and perception always as the all ways questioning man in the center of every answer. The human thinks we are thinking calmly wanting answers the anthropomorphic Anthropocene. The man puts himself at the center of words of meaning of all life and autistics always yearn for more and deeper connections that suppers wanting synesthesia as the main meal in reasoning towards all ways wanting for the people to feel. Always appetite and thirst for more understanding must swim in the synesthetic ways that waters come closest to describing.

(Wolfond, forthcoming)

Autistic languaging (which is always bodying in relation) is characterized by neurotypicals as automatism, gibberish. "Bathing" in language (Adam's word), repeating letters on YouTube so they vibrate, the early typing of "red jar" and "green frog," were never considered descriptive enough for "clear" communication. Hyperlexia, an early ability to decipher letters and numbers and read exceptionally early as Adam did before he could walk,[15] is rarely discussed as synesthetic, proprioceptive bodying-languaging, but rather, as a dysfunctional anomaly whereby autistic hyperlexics cannot instrumentalize language. Neurotypicality's fixity demands we sit still; mirrored in language's grammatical order; grammar excises the immediate, the excess and it may be that the poet and artist can return us to it. Adam challenges this body-word-world order, unapologetic for the way he writes,

I expect people will try to read how I write as it is doing the hate of autistics by liberating autistic language placing our ways pacing into the way of perception and language I am all about and I am good at it and I know that people forget that I can write in my own language.

(Wolfond, forthcoming)

He leads us through "fast rushing rivers of talkers," streams, wells and eddies that is the way language, bodies and the world's moves because "[the] appetite and thirst for more understanding must swim in the synesthetic ways that waters come closest to describing" (forthcoming). We must swim also in the way the words emerge from index finger to device, remembering also how difficult it is to add punctuation (which requires him to switch to a different screen), when it is hard enough to type out each feeling word gushing forth. In his forthcoming book, Adam takes his affiliations with water to the next level. "Like water I am," a poem he wrote two years ago, now flows into deeper understandings of how the body languages, which cannot be separated from the becoming of experience itself.

> I want to talk about my experience passing as a reader. . . . I could read letters and words when I was still a [an] infant . . . the words vibrate colors and sounds and the way I rally words brings up the way I started to see them, and using words for conversation wells the way I saturate in the words. . . . The way I language is the way I feel the words, and the way I think about them as alive, and the way open letters dance, wanting words that language for pleasure. The way language moves thinking, naming feelings so complex, and I can't always describe the way I know it, but I can tell how I dance with it.
>
> (Wolfond, forthcoming)

This is the "art" that is the "open way," a "dancing for the answering" (Wolfond, forthcoming) moving with "the walls that are never still" (Wolfond, 2019, p. 36), "able to scatter/the sound of yellow fortuitous/trombones are honking/the dance of yellow . . ." (ibid, 41) – "making art that goes towards missing words" (ibid, 40), "master[fully] 'ticcing'" (ibid, 38), towards "tall ideas [. . . that are] the open way of thinking/that use the patterns of the way/I motion with language" (ibid, 18):

> The ways of water is the pace of thinking, wanting to pool, wanting to rush, wanting to rain, wanting to fast flow rivers, wanting to fall, wanting to saturate, wanting to dance always through my fingers, wanting to teach the ways of movement.
>
> (Wolfond, forthcoming)

The relational-motional (Manning & Massumi, 2014) as a way of study and a collaborative artistic practice is important to us for creation and invention; every move in relation, every object, alive in the dance. We propose that to live together diversely, and to think about care and mutual influence in the care network, we must open and attune to all ways of bodily and relational expression that exceed and extend the predetermined forms established not only by academic research, but also, by the social rules that prescribe how we should communicate, move and relate. Because languaging is also relational-motional, this way of writing merges with our experimental, processual artistic practice.

How does this kind of experimental play facilitate encounters that can detour the systemic injustices that have excluded Adam and other autistic speaking and non-speaking bodies from participation in all facets of society? How can we recognize these encounters through neurodiverse ways?

How do we add *back in* what academic and capital forms expect us to delete for clarity and efficiency? How do we return to relation? Ralph Savarese writes, "[i]f one thing is clear, neurotypicals struggle to understand forms of being very different from their own" (in Manning, 2020, p. 275). Yet if one thing is certain, we need different ways of knowing and relating.

Walking movement is important in our artistic practice. We walk with sticks, think about how the body spaces space (as in proprioception) and how we language. In the photo in Figure 3.3, we transferred Adam's excerpt "Wet" onto porous cheesecloth and took it for a walk in the ice and snow, noticing the trails that words left behind.[16] The cheesecloth is typically used in cooking to merge the flavor of ingredients into a stew or broth. It is in the merging that the emergence of something *more* occurs. Leaving marks of ink behind in the process of moving, like footprints and paths we make, the words begin to come apart in contact with the water, bleeding into each other, becoming with the ice and snow. Instead of parsing this relation, we continue adding, the damp cloth collecting particles of the ground. Like the synesthetic-proprioceptive experience of moving, writing and feeling – the emergent nature of intrarelation – Adam questions the impermanence of the bodies and words that move otherwise in transition – in contrast to utilitarian words that totalize autism and autistic experience as pathology.

When we think of participation – not as an adjunct to already-established forms that distance the relation between researcher and subject, but as fully engaged processes – what emerges is something that cannot be predetermined.[17] Languaging becomes a *thinkingfeeling* through poetry and oscillating sticks. Sticks, rubber bath toys, like transducers, are dousing the field to feel. Adam's sentences undulate, waves landing then folding over-under, summoning the immediate and all-at-once motions of his typing finger to the keyboard, the thinkingfeeling, the context, the associations forging forth. Recalling Audre Lorde's writing on "the master's language" in the excerpt earlier, Adam asks us to recognize what is indigenous to autistic languaging[18] for autistics are otherwise forced in rehabilitative programs to order their bodies and sentences, and to explain why they do things the way they do in the ways (and language) neurotypicals can understand. Autistics are called to speak even when they cannot, and despite learning to type or use other devices to communicate, are continually suspect for their need of support (which is entirely connected and relational). Ableist questions about intradependence, authorship, lack of speech . . . expect us to explain by parsing relation not only with each other, but with the ecological milieu that is also collaborating. When Adam asks "can a good body feel without another body?" and comments, "I base my pace on you," he is commenting on both the human and the nonhuman affects, the pace of the *atmospheres* to which he aligns, and

Figure 3.3 Experiment with calligraphy, walking, Adam's excerpt "Wet Words,"
lake water and ice, 2020.

also, the support he needs from me and others. Languaging as autistic
expression in relation and as artistic process – "really into the seething
good cracks of wanting thought" (2019, p. 28) – is always emergent, on
the move and towards "the open way of telling."[19]

Notes

1 Milieu suggests to be in the midst of the middle. It also suggests environment. We use milieu as it also suggests being in the midst of movement as transitions are keenly perceived by Adam, and can sometimes take more time and effort to move through.

2 We find the invisible felt and objects also an important part of pacing relation as well as physical human bodies.

3 Adam also thinks in immediate terms. For example, if we are to ask him if he wants something and we haven't specified it for later, he will assume the proposal is for the immediate moment.

4 This is not experienced by all autistic people in the same way but seems to be experienced more so by those who would have been in the past labeled "classically autistic" – and those who are non-speaking. However, such an attunement to different ways of perception perhaps makes us more open to understanding the movements of others.

5 In addition to autism, Adam has been diagnosed with "tic disorder," yet again, we wish to avoid medical and pathologized language for understanding diverse modes of perception – modes that are negatively compared to "normal" perception and movement. We acknowledge that the better way is to suggest that there is a majority way of perception, and also, minority ways which therefore does not diminish them.

6 A stim is a reclaimed term from behavioral psychology: "self-stimulatory behavior." Some in the autism community refer to stims as pleasurable and also for coping. Adam also suggests that ticcing-stimming are co-operative.

7 Sometimes, there's no time for the explanatory comma that has preceded so much work on autism and neurodivergence, particularly creative work that thinks outside of systemic meanings of what we have imagined as inclusion and accessibility that are underpinned by neurotypical forms of embodiment and expression that signify meaning about autism. Disrupting institutionalized methods that are predetermined, we need to return to relation and movement rhizomatically, nonhierarchically, which is how we began this work in 2016 – derived from years of dealing with barriers to inclusion. In what I call our collaborative dissertation: *Neurodiversity in Relation: an artistic intraethnography* (2020), we write that the term neurodiversity is transient and ever moving; its meanings will morph over time, a new word and new understandings will emerge. In our work, we use neurodiverse, neurodivergent and autistic and acknowledge their nuanced meanings that have transpired over time (see also: esteerelation.com). We suggest that identity language, although it has been important to move neurodiversity and reclaim autism from the clinical vice, struggles with direction and positionality. We wriggle from fixed positions. This is not how Adam situates or orients. Rather, he's interested in movement. Neurodiverse is therefore used in our work as a gesture for way. Autistic is the signpost to remember autism's clinical roots and then reclamation of its meaning by autistic people. Neurodivergent is used in recognition of individuals who diverge from neurotypicality but who do not necessarily identify as autistic, thus creating a new direction for thinking about diversity "because even autistics, who are most definitely neurodivergent, are diverse in an infinity of ways that expand from the neurological . . . the adjective neurodiverse [reminds us that] we need a new concept for diversity within diversity that isn't measured by the standard of typicality" (SenseLab, 2018).

Neurotypicality suggests fixity –position, attitude and measures for an ideal that is also described as normality. We write that neurotypicality and neoliberalism also operate for each other. Open and *all ways*, is how Adam writes it. Ways suggests more than one way of being and becoming in the world and which does not always orient to the vertical, horizontal. In autistic perception to which many "classical autistics" describe – which merges proprioception and synesthesia – there are multiple motional objectiles to be tendrilled through in order to move "I line to your pace." Adam writes of lining in multiple ways with objects, people, sounds . . . so we adopted the term *aligning* to denote continual movement to find one's way through, or a way of thinking about object-full (objectile) transitions. This is a perception that perceives the "unfiltered detail" – or what Manning and Massumi refer to as the relational-motional or what Adam and I refer to as the visual field (vision is more than sight) that is always moving. Our work is all about enmeshment with the way of Adam's perception, relation, languaging, de-forming in the world.

8 We refer to neurotypical architectures as the way space is arranged for economic production, and also, consider how this influences the way bodies move and the way work is formed. A school rubric for a ministry curriculum, for example, maintains normative expectations of the able, speaking, independent body. It situates me, falsely, as the more able and therefore directive body in the support dyad.

9 When experience is so vastly different than the vertical-horizontal "orientations" that still imply fixity, we continue to leave out the immersive experience and movement of neurodiverse ways and relational bodies. We erase the integral support systems that are always there. Adam and I have been reading all work by Robert MacFarlane who understands interconnectedness and also the deletions that research makes: "This is the frothy . . . network that underlies and interconnects all scientific knowledge but about which we so rarely say anything" (2019, pp. 108–109). "I have this plan," adds his colleague, "that for each formal scientific paper I ever publish I will also write its dark twin, its underground mirror piece – the true story of how the data for that cooked, tidy hypothesis-evidence-proof paper actually got acquired" (ibid).

10 Arakawa and Gins also think about space and architecture as either delimiting or potentiating movement; they create new spaces, such as Bioscleaves House, where thinking about movement deliberately is a way of staying alive: "how not to die" (See references on Arakawa and Gins and Arakawa, 1994, 2002, 2014). Following pre-constructed paths where we no longer have to think about our bodies is the way of stasis, death. Other artists also explore space and movement differently, and I think of the Situationists, the Fluxus movement here, although Adam and I, with our other artist-collaborator, Ellen Bleiwas, and previously, Kyla Brown, have studied artistic works of ritual, repetition, mobile architecture, ice works and more. These artistic movements also rethink neoliberal spaces that limit our movements and ability to relate with our environment as well as with each other.

11 Artist Lygia Clark (See: Suely Rolnik, no date) suggests that our life, artworking is our oeuvre which is therefore a lifetime of thinking-feeling and studying together. Studying is our word in place of research as it implies the artistic process more than object and form; studying is the process of relation. Both Fred Moten and Erin Manning use this concept in similar ways, understanding that the university is in decline, finding other s/paces to invent differently (see

Manning, 2020; Harney & Moten, 2019). Studying is an affirmation also of collaboration, process and creation that can happen anywhere – beyond institutional walls. Drawing on Moten's work, Manning writes, "Thought irreducible to practice moves outside the registers of categorization, shifting the conditions of the undercommon ways of cawing. We don't need the university for this – in fact, the university often closes down the registers of sociality this mode of study needs to thrive" (Manning, 2020, p. 223). Study isn't innobled, says Moten (ibid), but embedded within our playful, speculative, experimental practices. From this, we may access various texts in philosophy, anthropology, literature, art and so on. Neurodiverse ways bring forth not only conditions for studying together, but for rethinking how and what we need to study.

12 Before Adam was supported with my hand on his back, he needed more support by withholding his forearm from the keyboard to provide weighted resistance so he could feel and pace his own movement. This was required as Adam indicated he had troubles feeling his body parts and had to think deliberately about where his limbs were in space. I would often breathe also like a metronome also to give rhythmic input so he could sustain his movement to sentence. At times, I am able to simply sit beside Adam, providing the relational "weight" he needs to feel his body to type.

13 We are entangled, mutual, and avoid "capture" to explore neurodiverse ways of relation and collective care not necessarily valued in our culture. Autistic expression, be in movement through the body or bodying through language (languaging) is considered disordered or dysfunctional. Adam's early experiences of language – synesthetic-hyperlexic self-learning of letters, words, numbers before he could walk, is viewed as non-instrumental. "I want milk" is more efficient than an orientation to emotional associations conjured by "red jar" and "green frog." But what would happen if we envisioned language acquisition and understanding that is entered through an entirely different door? Perhaps the efficient instrumentality of the English language as we use it loses the possibilities for expressing the richness of relation? So we resist capture in every sense (particularly as the senses also tend to be parsed) as much as autistic perception resists categorization and classification in neurotypical language. Autistic perception, ways of "seeing" and languaging, questions orientation, the way we "see" and move in the world, and thus the way of care and support. Where do bodies begin and end? Who/what supports who/what? These are questions that cannot be answered as we are carried and influenced by multiple bodies in relation, and also a body boundary which Adam and some other autistics have written, literally cannot feel: "I can sometimes feel my legs but not the ground of my feet" (Wolfond, 2016). The world is felt in the pacing duration *au milieu*. Movement is the way Adam feels and many or our explorations move with sticks, go on walks, jump in and out of the seat while typing. Proprioception – the way of spacing space, and feeling-moving-merging the senses through it, "queers" the way of moving and seeing (understanding that "seeing" extends beyond the eyes). Queering is the "slanting space" with sticks "and a watching of radical thinking" (see Klar & Wolfond, 2019). Adam literally cannot always feel his body in space without a weighted object, a waving – or what he calls "twallowing" stick – or a toy to tap as he walks; he writes about how he blurs the visual field in order to move through it. Permanent fixity unsettles while movement as "flying" and "landing" thoughts, and movements, is the way: dis assembly.

14 This arises from behavioral and other therapies that have attempted to capture and control Adam, incarcerate him, and blame me for not rehabilitating Adam to become more "functional" and (neurotypically) independent (see Douglas & Klar, 2020).

15 While Adam is non-speaking, he is able to read some words and phrases aloud and can read if I help his eyes follow paragraphs along a page. Otherwise, the words begin to dance and move on the page, which makes reading otherwise difficult. Adam and I instead read together every day, and he also listens to podcasts and lectures.

16 Sometimes Adam's prose and poetry lead me to enact concepts with materials. Other times, as in the exhibition at the beginning of this chapter, Adam envisages how we should experiment and move with materials. We are in a constant state of motion with ideas.

17 Avoiding fixity, phenomenology isn't our method as it seeks to separate inside subjective experience from the outside. "[Phenomenology . . .] separates the human from the animal and from its given objects as it tries to reconcile them with experience," writes Elizabeth Grosz, "Each assumes the functional or experiencing body as a given rather than an effect of process of continual creation, movement or individuation" (ibid, 2011, p. 29). It "parses the field in order to restore it" (Manning & Massumi, 2014). Individuation, as Brian Massumi writes, is a coming together in a morphogenetic relation; individuation is more than individual, challenging the way we think about identity and subjectivity and the manner of non/autistic writing and agency that is always made in relation. This is important because this is how autistic perception moves and relates. Phenomenology assumes the body and world are fixed – as in backgrounding the affective ecological milieu (middle) rather than being in the midst of relation. So the question isn't how autistic experience differs from neurotypical experience and how to extract that answer. Rather, Adam asks, "How can art think with neurodiversity?" and also, "can a good body feel without another body?" calling us towards the human and nonhuman bodies in process.

18 Ralph Savarese has termed this *Autistext*.

19 Manning and SenseLab at Concordia University name this schizzanarchiving. It "is a call for a practice of transversal collectivity. It is a political call for the creation of minor socialities that resist reorganizing according to predetermined categories. We do not fit (ourselves) into transversal collectivities. Events call us to merge into the body-earth compositions" (2020, 315). Anarchiving practices emerge in relation, not an archiving . . . "it is a culling that pulls from a future a tendency, an orientation on process. The registering of the minor catapults time's linearity. From a line grows a spiral. What is felt in the catapulting is potential" (ibid).

References

Arakawa. Gins, M. (March 2014). *The Funambulist Pamphets*. Edited by Leopold Lambert, Punctum Books.

Barad, K. (2012). Interview with Karen Barad. In R. Dolphijn & I. van der Tuin (Eds.), *New materialism: Interviews and cartographies*. Ann Arbor, MI: Open Humanities Press.

Douglas, P., & Klar, E. (2020). Beyond disordered brains and mother blame: Critical issues in autism and mothering. In L. O'Brien Hallstein, A. O'Reilly, & M.

Vandenbeld Giles (Eds.), *The Routledge companion to motherhood*. London and New York: Routledge.

Gins, M. Arakawa. (2002). *Architectural Body*. The University of Alabama Press.

Gins, M. (1994). *Helen Keller or Arakawa*. Burning Books with East-West Cultural Studies.

Grosz, E. (2011). *Becoming undone: Darwinian reflections on life, politics, art*. Durham, NC & London: Duke University Press.

Harney, S., & Moten, F. (2019). *The undercommons: Fugitive planning & black study*. Wivenhoe & New York: Port Watson.

Klar, E. (2019). *esteerelation.com*.

Klar, E. (2020). *Neurodiversity in relation: An artistic intraethnography* [PhD Dissertation]. York University. Retrieved from https://yorkspace.library.yorku.ca/xmlui/handle/10315/37776

Klar, E., & Wolfond, A. (2019). *S/pace*. S/pace (open captions) on Vimeo.

MacFarlane, R. (2019). *Underland: A Deep Time Journey*. Hamish Hamilton: Penguin Books.

MacFarlane, R. (2013). *The old ways: a journey on foot*. Hamish Hamilton: Penguin Books.

Manning, E. (2020). *For a pragmatics of the useless*. Durham & London: Duke University Press.

Manning, E., & Massumi, B. (2014). *Thought in the act: Passages in the ecology of experience*. Minneapolis, MN: University of Minnesota Press.

Massumi, B. (2002). *Parables for the virtual*. Durham, NC & London: Duke University Press,.

Massumi, B. (2015). *The politics of affect*. Cambridge: Polity Press.

Rolnik, S. *Molding a contemporary soul: The empty-full of Lygia Clark*. Retrieved from http://caosmose.net/suelyrolnik/pdf/molding%20john_nadine.pdf

Savarese, R. (2012). Gobs and gobs of metaphor. *Inflexions* 5, "Simondon: Milieu, Techniques, Aesthetics" 184–223. Retrieved from www.inflexions.org

SenseLab. (2018). *Diversity in diversity*. Retrieved from http://senselab.ca/wp2/diversity-in-diversity-launch-sept-5-at-19h30-senselab/

Wolfond, A. (2016). *The aspects of talking and how I am like Moses*. Retrieved from https://vimeo.com/254603007

Wolfond, A. (2019). *In way of music water answers toward questions other than what is autism*. Minneapolis, MN: Unrestricted Editions.

Wolfond, A. (Forthcoming, 2021) *Open book in ways of water* (working title).

participatory videos with disability activists; a two-year photovoice project addressing paratransit barriers to improve quality of life; and more recently the use of digital storytelling to explore life stage transitions for youth with disabilities. All of these projects feature creative methods guided by the principles of participatory research in working alongside community. Using primarily visual media, the projects have all been longer than a year, which supported relationship building and pivoting as needed with iterative processes.

As an architect and social worker, Alison has 10 years of experience working alongside the disability community in the areas of accessible housing, inclusive community design, and disability policy. Working within community disability agencies, she employed participatory design programs with disabled persons to envision and transform their homes and communities based on their unique experiences and needs. The results of our work have influenced legislation changes, informed policy around programming and services, and raised awareness about the challenges and injustices disabled persons must navigate on a daily basis.

However, what happens when group participation becomes inaccessible? When the act of coming together represents an overwhelming idea for individuals keen to participate, yet unclear how to do so when participation requires interacting as a group? What does access mean in these

Figure 4.1 Image from Love Bytes: Stories about the Right to Love video. As part of a participatory video research study completed in 2012 in Calgary, Alberta. All 14 videos from the project can be accessed on the Disability Action Hall www.actionhall.ca/2010/12/love-bytes-stories-about-right-to-love.html

4 When participatory approaches are inaccessible

A movement toward research engagement through multi-sensory storytelling

Kathleen C. Sitter and Alison L. Grittner

Introduction

Over the last few decades, there has been a growing interest in participatory visual media, such as drawing, photography, and video. Taken up in collaborative settings, creative forms of expression serve as a mode of inquiry, an approach to meaning-making, and a way of knowing. When working alongside disabled activists and community members, collaborative-based approaches are encouraged for the inclusiveness they provide. Participatory approaches espouse the strengths and benefits associated with group-based methodologies that are community focused. These include elements such as collaboration, connection, collective empowerment, democratic engagement, and mitigating power imbalances. The process of explaining knowledge through photographs and videos and connecting with others can be a validating and transformative experience. Self and group empowerment, critical consciousness and the cycles of dialogue, reflection, and action are well documented in the literature (see Reason & Bradbury, 2006), and are considered core elements of participatory action research. Indeed, when critical theories guide participatory-based research, the process informs praxis that strives for inclusivity, agency, and choice while honoring tacit knowledge. Participatory action research is generally defined as working alongside communities in research that emphasizes participation and action. It involves collaboration, seeking to understand the world in order to change it, and is grounded in lived experience and reflection, which we will discuss in greater detail later.

In this chapter, we speak from our experiences as community-based researchers. For the last 17 years, Kathleen's research has predominantly involved the application of arts-based media in participatory action research studies working alongside disabled activists. Previous participatory research included: a 12-month community-based project about sexual rights creating

Figure 4.2 Design and renovation of Edda and Amir's house in Calgary, Alberta, Canada. Undertaken as part of RAD Renovations, a participatory design program at Accessible Housing Calgary, started by Alison L. Grittner in 2014. Photo credits: Alison L. Grittner and Accessible Housing Calgary.

contexts, and how do researchers honor the needs and desires of participants who appear to be in conflict with underlying assumptions associated with the philosophical foundations of participatory research designs? Within our own practice and research, we have witnessed – and at times, admittedly, supported – barriers that include communication methods that privilege spoken and written discourse, assuming participants feel safe and comfortable in group environments, expecting participants to travel to locations determined by the researcher, and institutional and funding expectations that arts-based findings be translated into traditional written reports.

With consideration to the social, political, and physical contexts, this chapter explores opening up participatory informed research that creates space for individual engagement, whereby individuals are invited to engage with research processes in modalities that best suit their unique strengths and experiences. It begins with the description of action research and its importance in critical disability research, a framework that critiques disabling structures and positions disability as a diverse and complex experience (Sitter & Nusbaum, 2018). Then we share some challenges that arose from a two-year participatory action research study involving a group of activists exploring the topic of transportation using photovoice. The second part of the chapter includes an exploration on the role of engagement in research and the need to embrace multisensory storytelling through a critical disability lens in order to amplify and enact change through different ways of knowing.

Action research

Action research focuses on the experience and understanding of people who are centrally involved in the issues being explored (Stringer, 2007). While it includes a family of approaches, there are key characteristics such as goals of social change and relational processes (Wallerstein & Duran, 2003). Kemmis and McTaggart (2005) also identified several core tenets that include participation, collaboration, emancipation, and critical exploration of power. Action research is also important from a critical disability orientation, understanding the intersections of disability identities, ableist attitudes, structures, and systems, and the role of rights in social citizenships and full participation in society (Meekosha & Shuttleworth, 2009; Pothier & Devlin, 2006). When disability intersects with other social locations – such as racialization, precarious immigration statuses, non-heteronormative sexual identities, and aging – inequities significantly increase. The lives of individuals with disabilities are also massively shaped by institutions, attitudes, and social and historical understandings (Grace, 2020). Indeed, there has been an ongoing emphasis to engage in participatory and emancipatory research working alongside disabled people due to the focus on self-empowerment, agency, and shared decision-making throughout the research design. When arts-based methods are involved, it also unlocks further opportunities for unique forms of expression.

Participatory action research: challenges of inclusion and access

The collaborative undercurrents of participatory models require people to physically gather as a group. Ironically, this can also exclude people. For instance, the first author of this chapter, Kathleen, was involved in a two-year participatory action research study using photovoice that explored the topic of transportation as a social determinant of health. The findings were subsequently shared online and through community exhibits. While initially designed as a group-based format, the process also evolved into several one-to-one settings, based on the needs of participants. Originally, the group had planned to come together every other week and share photographs that explored the topic of quality of life and transportation. The community partner had secured accessible space and transportation. While the activists knew one another for years, several found this task of coming together to talk and share photos daunting; social gatherings were outside of their comfort level. Transportation to the meetings was also challenging for some of the participants. Para-transit service provided a one-hour pick-up window of 30 minutes before and after their designated pick-up times, and would only wait five minutes for individuals to be ready. At times, people would come to the meeting distraught, or decide they could not go through this ordeal of uncertain wait times and rushing to board. Further, participants were challenged by the dynamics of participation, which privileged verbal discussion. While some people brought photographs that were very powerful, some individuals were reticent to speak or provide context about their photographs in a group setting, and in photovoice, narrative is a core aspect of the methodology. As a researcher, Kathleen was responsible for creating the agenda and ensuring opportunities for participation across the group. Based on how the process unfolded, Kathleen and the participants collaboratively reworked the design so people could attend and participate in different formats that included both group and individual engagement, resulting in a participation style that was more in line with the spirit of participatory action research. This included both individual and group-based meetings.

This example highlights potential issues employing group-based methods. The reliance on articulating and agreeing upon themes in a shared space can be problematic for several reasons. In photovoice, participatory data gathering primarily focuses on talking. As the researcher, choosing a method that privileges participation among those comfortable and at ease with verbal processing overshadows participatory design goals. Additionally, arts-based methods like photovoice possess access issues if they disproportionately weigh the analysis on verbal discourse: while photovoice holds participant's visual stories at the core, it continues to privilege the spoken word in analysis, and relies on the written narrative to provide context to the audience when viewing the photograph. While the visual is inherently tethered to the verbal, this approach to analysis and knowledge dissemination holds an imbalance that problematizes participation. With these considerations, we examine the need to shift our focus from participation to one that emphasizes the act of engagement.

The research turn of engagement

How might we explore the practice of centering disability in qualitative inquiry? While innovative participatory practices are essential, we posit that the practice of centering disability in qualitative inquiry also requires a focus on engagement and holding onto an awareness that writing and talking as dominant discourses in communicating also privilege certain ways of data gathering. Indeed, ableist norms exist throughout research processes, including pre-determining group vs. individual data-collection, requiring text and verbal explanations of arts-based materials, privileging theoretical knowledge over experiential and arts-based knowing, and emphasizing textual modes of knowledge mobilization exemplified by traditional academic journals. If we are to truly respond to the call for engaging with disability justice agendas within qualitative inquiry, we must reconceptualize what it means to value different ways in which we come to know and experience the world through all of our senses. Touch. Taste. Smell. Sound. Sight. In doing so, it is not for the researcher to transpose these modes into written text, but for the researcher to explore ways in which to engage in participatory data collection, analysis, and knowledge translation through multi-sensory modes.

We believe engagement should take precedence over the focus of collaborative designs in order to enact different forms of knowing in research through a critical disability lens. When researchers are tethered to institutions, they inherently hold power due to their expert status and also must answer to Institutional Review Boards (IRBs). Participatory researchers are charged with defining participation parameters and ensuring their practices are guided by democratic principles, while ultimately responsible for any risk participants might experience. Thus, we must ask if power can truly be mitigated in the participatory research process when it is connected to the academic institution, as these challenges are inherent for many action researchers guided by popular education theories. While co-researcher roles are malleable at various points throughout the research process (Herr & Anderson, 2005), this does not negate certain defined responsibilities outlined by the academy, which will always rest with the primary researcher. When participatory research methodologies are connected to an academic institution, we think it is critical for researchers to be transparent surrounding their agendas and power. This involves sharing both their institutional responsibilities and goals for the research with participants, and working from an ethics of care positionality throughout the process.

Further, if we attempt to pivot the discussion of participation to one of engagement, this would also amplify different forms of knowledge and shift the emphasis to include ways people can share how they live, experience, and know things in the world. To do so, ideal formats for expressing and sharing knowledges must be informed by individuals themselves. The role of researchers must include creating space for people to engage, share, and understand in order to emphasize perspectives that privilege these research engagements throughout the research process – from data gathering through to knowledge translation.

Researchers must ask: how can space be created to engage all ways of knowing? In their participatory inquiry paradigm, Heron and Reason talk about four different ways of knowing: experiential knowing, propositional knowing, presentational knowing, and practical knowing (2008). Experiential knowing is tacit and relational, and occurs through an encounter with a person, place, or thing; propositional knowing is knowing in intellectual terms through theories, facts, and statements; presentational knowing is knowing through expressive imaginal space and creative storytelling; and practical knowing is knowing through doing. All these forms of knowledge are intertwined, yet we often privilege propositional knowledge in Western research. A call for innovative engagement practices that draw on all of the senses in understanding experiences and knowledges is needed. This will require a stronger focus on both experiential and presentational knowledge specifically because those forms of knowledge creation are commonly overlooked. Multisensory storytelling holds potential for engaged research that embraces experiential and presentational knowing.

Knowing through the senses: multi-sensory storytelling in research

Historically, disabled voices have been excluded from decision-making that impacts their lives (Biggs & Carter, 2016; Pulli, 2013). As most research privileges speaking and writing methods in understanding lived experiences, this inherently creates participation barriers for many disabled people, some of whom experience heightened sensory experiences in their interactions within the world (Grace, 2020). These include disabilities from autism spectrum disorder (Crane, Goddard, & Pring, 2009) to dementia (Day, Carreon, & Stump, 2000). Ignoring embodied experiences in the context of understanding the lives of disabled people risks overlooking core information in creating inclusive and participatory research environments.

How can our senses inform the development of inclusive research methods? How can we develop inclusive processes that incorporate multisensory data and audience engagement? Multi-sensory storytelling addresses this concern by using elevated sensory engagement that invites both storytellers and audiences into the research process. Multi-sensory storytelling refers to life-stories we look at, listen to, smell and taste, feel and experience (Fornefeld, 2013). There is substantive interest in the sensory experience across anthropology (Pink, 2011; Clifford & Marcus, 1986), cultural studies (Butler, 2006), commerce (Spence, 2015), public health (Williams & Swierad, 2019), and sociology (Drobnick, 2011; Howes, 2018). Examples of sensory methods include visual genres such as video, photography, digital stories, and cellphilms that represent experiences through multimodal imagery (Pink, 2011). Smells can signify an intense form of intimacy with a person or place, where olfactory methods such as smellwalks have been used to associate smells with experience and inspire reflection upon how a sense of community can develop from a mix of identities (Pink, 2011).

Although blended sensory methods are emergent, several promising examples include soundscape compositions in connecting to place-based experiences (Pink, 2015). Sensory ethnography combines visual media with sound to explore and represent a phenomenon (Pink, 2015). In olfactory methods, Sissel Tolaas's seminal work in urban smellscapes and sensory maps include extended periods of consultations, sensory walks, collecting and analyzing odors, mapping, interviews, and community involvement to explore affective meanings and emotional attachments to smells (Drobnick, 2011). Using headspace technology, she re-represents smells in her exhibitions, which have acted as a catalyst toward collective action amongst constituents who associate themselves and their activities with the smells they described (Drobnick, 2011). Multi-sensory method integration with olfactory stimuli, as well as gustatory, tactile, and visual cues are useful in understanding flavor perception (Spence, 2015). Sensory stories are also examples of interweaving images, text, and touch to convey a narrative (Grace, 2020; Forenefeld, 2013). Auditory methods, such as soundscapes, communicate sounds in relation to environments, and invite understanding of experiences through listening to others' sonic everyday (Pink, 2011).

However, sensory research methods have primarily not been used with disabled people (Grace, 2020). The, albeit limited, sensory research projects involving disabled persons to date have identified benefits in terms of mental well-being, self-expression, and awareness of talents (Grace, 2020). Examples of these methods are exhibited through the sensory projects (www. thesensoryprojects.co.uk) run by Joana Grace, which includes a series of projects and multisensory stories for disabled people. Another example includes the Interact Center in the United States (www.interactcenter.org), a visual arts studio and theater company with commissioned art work and exhibitions that have an active Instagram page @interactcenterarts including regular online exhibits, interviews, and Q&As. While these examples are not research focused, they provide possibilities for ways in which research designs that include disabled persons' lived experiences can be developed as engagement with sensory storytelling. Sensory stories combine touch, sound, and images to convey a narrative that enables people to create works of art. Countering ableist norms in research through sensory storytelling methods holds powerful possibilities for disabled individuals to benefit in terms of enjoyment, mental well-being, and self-expression, while generating awareness of their talents (Grace, 2020; Fornefeld, 2013).

Multi-sensory storytelling is an innovative research design in general, and specifically in the areas of disability and access. It builds on the biopsychosocial model of understanding social problems through first-person accounts (Grace, 2020). It calls for attending to the creation, engagement, and enactment of stories with disabled persons (Fornefeld, 2013). Doing so requires rethinking predominant and often exclusionary research designs through notions of multisensorality that prioritize first-person experiences through the elicitation of multiple senses (Pink, 2015). Understanding how, when, and why multisensory storytelling could be used as a research methodology, and the benefits and limitations of this approach in practice, requires exploring how different augmented senses are experienced through intertwined sensory channels (Pink, 2011). For example, multisensory storytelling that combines aural recordings with imagery – such as soundscapes with photographs, or an audio-video recording – is multisensorial: researchers, participants, and others who experience these recordings are sensorily emplaced and can "empathetically imagine" (Pink, 2011, p. 9) the creators' holistic sensory experiences, not merely the visual and aural aspects. Returning to the earlier example of the research project concerning transportation, perhaps having participants respond to their photography with soundscapes as an alternative to verbal and textual narratives would have added further modalities to the already rich first-person accounts and would have provided a more accessible format for engagement and ultimately gained a deeper understanding to the dimensions associated with the topic of inquiry.

Multisensory storytelling requires further ethical consideration concerning how participants are impacted by sharing their sensory experiences and memories. Communicating one's knowledge of living in the world and imagining the future is an inherently different experience of intimacy and exposure than sharing a textual narrative. Researchers using multisensory storytelling methods will require transparency and collaboration with participants, maintaining an open dialogue throughout the research process concerning their sensory storytelling choices and experiences. A core skill for researchers will be how they hold onto and honor the sensorial space, and do not transpose the multisensory knowledge into written prose. This raises key questions of how researchers can ethically engage in this form of inquiry while balancing academic requirements. It is not for researchers to transpose this knowledge into text.

The IRB process will necessitate institutional discussions and advocacy concerning how sensory methods can level the playing field for participants with varying abilities to contribute and ensure their voices, bodies, and knowledge are driving research.

Conclusions

In reflecting on the power of the senses, we came across an online article in *Critical Correspondence*, a publication of Movement Research about artistic practice in the context that surrounds the field of dance. Several dancers were interviewed about the boundaries of touch particularly during the pandemic. In highlighting the power of touch, one individual said, "So during the pandemic, excuse me, current pandemic, I noticed that I really wanna give hugs or high fives or fist bumps. And because of social distancing and possible transference (I don't know what the proper term for that is), but I am unable to do that. In general, touch, because it's one of our five senses, sometimes it feels like that sense is currently lost. If that makes sense" (Graczyk, Gabriel, W, M, & M, 2020). How we interact, communicate in the world and connect with one another is done through all of our senses. They hold our knowledge, and impact who we are.

Participatory approaches to research seek to embed inclusivity, agency, and shared decision-making within the research process. Critical disability research has embraced these participatory, emancipatory, and arts-based research designs with the goal of creating inclusive knowledge. Yet these research methods often continue to privilege ableist methods of knowing and communicating. This includes emphasizing verbal and textual sharing and analysis, as well as defining community and collaboration as physically gathering in a group. Qualitative research that embraces disability justice agendas must reconsider diverse ways of knowing. Shifting the focus within disability research from participation to engagement involves expanding ways of knowing to include experiential and presentational modalities, such as multisensory storytelling. Multisensorial research designs allow disabled persons to share non-textual narratives and their embodied experiences through sensory art.

When designing and conducting disability justice research, we encourage researchers to reflect and consider the ableist undercurrents that remain unquestioned within research methodologies and methods, especially those labelled as collaborative and emancipatory. What do research methods, analysis, and knowledge translation involve when written and verbal communication is removed? How can we design research collaboratively that engages participants' strengths, multi-dimensional ways of knowing, and sensory experiences? Engagement research through multi-sensory storytelling holds great potential to unfold different ways of knowing and will inherently yield new ways of understanding lived experiences while centering disability in qualitative inquiry.

References

Biggs, E. E., & Carter, E. W. (2016). Quality of life for transition-age youth with autism or intellectual disability. *Journal of Autism and Developmental Disorders, 46*, 190–204.

Butler, T. (2006). A walk of art: The potential of the sound walk as practice in cultural geography. *Social and Cultural Geography, 6*, 889–908.

Clifford, J., & Marcus, G. E. (1986). *Writing culture: The poetics and politics of ethnography.* Berkeley, CA: University of California Press.

Crane, L., Goddard, L., & Pring, L. (2009). Sensory processing in adults with autism spectrum disorders. *Autism, 13*(3), 215–228.

Day, K., Carreon, D., & Stump, C. (2000). The therapeutic design of environments for people with dementia: A review of the empirical research. *The Gerontologist, 40*(4), 397–416.

Drobnick, J. (2011). The city, distilled. In M. Diaconu, E. Heuberger, R. Mateus-Berr, & L. M. Vosicky (Eds.), *Senses and the city: An interdisciplinary approach to urban sensescapes* (pp. 257–275). Germany: Lit Verlag.

Fornefeld, B. (2013). Storytelling with all our senses: Mehr-Sinn® Geschichten. In N. Grove (Ed.), *Using storytelling to support children and adults with special needs: Transforming lives through telling tales* (pp. 78–85). New York, NY: Routledge.

Grace, J. (2020). *Multisensory rooms: Myth busting the magic.* New York, NY: Routledge.

Graczyk, B., Gabriel, A., W, M., M, D., M, J. (2020, October 8). *Boundaries of touch: Beth Graczyk, Aaron Gabriel, Michael W, Daniel M, and Jule M.* Retrieved October 8, 2020, from https://movementresearch.org/publications/critical-correspondence/boundaries-of-touch-beth-aaron-daniel-michael-jule

Heron, J., & Reason, P. (2008). Extended epistemology within a co-operative inquiry (2nd ed.). In P. Reason & H. Bradbury (Eds.), *The SAGE handbook of action research* (pp. 366–380). Los Angeles, CA: Sage Publications.

Herr, K., & Anderson, G. L. (2005). *The action research dissertation: A guide for students and faculty.* Thousand Oaks, CA: Sage Publications.

Howes, D. (Ed.). (2018). *Senses and sensation: Critical and primary sources: History and sociology.* London: Bloomsbury.

Kemmis, S., & McTaggart, R. (2005). Participatory action research: Communicative action and the public sphere. In N. K. Denzin & Y. S. Lincoln (Eds.), *The Sage handbook of qualitative research* (3rd ed., pp. 559–604). Thousand Oaks, CA: Sage Publications.

Meekosha, H., & Shuttleworth, R. (2009). What's so "critical" about critical disability studies? *Australian Journal of Human Rights, 15*(1), 47–76.

Pink, S. (2011). A multisensory approach to visual methods. In E. Margolis & L. Pauwels (Eds.), *The SAGE handbook of visual research methods* (pp. 601–614). Thousand Oaks, CA: Sage Publications.

Pink, S. (2015). *Doing sensory ethnography* (2nd ed.). London: Sage Publications.

Pothier, D., & Devlin, R. (Eds.). (2006). *Critical disability theory: Essays in philosophy, politics, and law.* Vancouver, BC: UBC Press.

Pulli, T. (2013). Describing and evaluating the storytelling experience: A conceptual framework. In N. Grove (Ed.), *Using storytelling to support children and adults with special needs: Transforming lives through telling tales* (pp. 120–127). New York, NY: Routledge.

Reason, P., & Bradbury, H. (Eds.). (2006). *Handbook of action Research: The concise paperback edition.* London: Sage Publications.

Sitter, K. C., & Nusbaum, E. A. (2018). Critical disability studies and community engagement. In D. E. Lund (Ed.), *The Wiley international handbook of service-learning for social justice* (pp. 191–202). Hoboken, NJ: Wiley Blackwell.

Spence, C. (2015). Multisensory flavor perception. *Cell, 26,* 24–35.

Stringer, E. T. (2007). *Action research* (3rd ed.). Thousand Oaks, CA: Sage Publications.

Wallerstein, N. B., & Duran, B. (2003). The conceptual, historical, and practical roots of community-based participatory research and related participatory traditions. In M. Minkler & N. B. Wallerstein (Eds.), *Community-based participatory research in health* (pp. 27–52). San Francisco, CA: Jossey Bass.

Williams, O., & Swierad, E. M. (2019). A multisensory multilevel health education model for diverse communities. *International Journal of Environmental Research and Public Health, 16*(5), 872.

5 Inclusion, sign language, and qualitative research interviewing

Stephanie L. Kerschbaum

This chapter makes an argument for inclusivity in qualitative interview research, focusing on signing deaf participants and researchers. To ensure that signing participants are regularly part of research processes and the concomitant production of knowledge, it is essential for researchers to engage key challenges around sign language transcription and the labor that is required to attend to data that emerges in a signed interview or interaction. In laying out these challenges, the chapter further reaffirms that conducting inclusive qualitative research is not only about recruiting people from particular populations or groups but also creating conditions that can enable people's participation, a process that begins from the earliest moments of conceptualizing a study.

Perhaps the most apparent challenge involved in including signing deaf participants in interview research is that of language: if a researcher does not use a sign language, people who primarily communicate in sign language may not want to volunteer for an interview. If the researcher has not allocated funding for accessibility in their research budget, then deaf participants, even if they volunteer, may find themselves excluded from participating. If interviews are collected according to a uniform process, as is often recommended in interviewing textbooks, then anyone for whom that process is inaccessible will be excluded, a particular concern given the diversity of communicative practices among deaf people. Consequently, because researchers cannot know from the outset all of the communicative needs and practices of their potential participants, it is essential for those researchers to deepen their understanding of barriers that can constrain possibilities for knowledge generation.

To move toward inclusivity for signing deaf people in qualitative interview research, this chapter offers insights and lessons from my experiences generating data with disabled faculty as part of an interview study conducted between 2013 and 2016. As a deaf academic myself, it was crucial to me that signing deaf academics be part of this study given their significant underrepresentation in academia[1] as well as among deaf faculty,[2] not to mention the ideological forces of audism that constrain possibilities for many deaf academics (see, e.g., Harmon, 2010). I ultimately conducted four interviews with signing deaf academics. Because I regularly use sign language interpreting as a workplace accommodation, I was comfortable engaging in signed interviews even though I am not a fully fluent American Sign Language (ASL) user; this comfort was further aided by the fact that all the participants were skilled sign language users and/or speechreaders who readily adjusted to my communication style.[3]

Not only did I believe it was important to better understand the experiences of signing deaf faculty, but I was excited to do sign language interviews because I anticipated that working with sign language data would make it easier for me to move within the video-recorded data as I analyzed it. Sign language is a visual language that I can readily understand on video, so I reasoned that I would not have to pay the same kind of laborious attention that I do when listening to and analyzing oral interview data.[4] What I didn't realize until I started working with the sign language interviews, however, was just how much of a challenge it would be to move video recordings of sign language and its three-dimensional spatial and temporal modalities into the two-dimensional written domains that comprised much of my analysis and which were required for publishing the research.

In what follows, I describe some challenges of working with sign language during qualitative research interviews, focusing particularly on interview interactions. Despite the ready availability of various technologies for recording and working with video as well as the fact that having visual access to these interviews indeed facilitated some of my analytic movements with the video recordings, I have largely been stymied in analyzing and writing about these interviews. I conclude by posing some ethical questions for researchers committed to creating more inclusive knowledge generation practices.

Challenge 1: How should researchers transcribe sign language interaction when transcription practices vary widely and there are few accepted conventions for moving sign language into written forms that facilitate interactional analysis?

As a deaf researcher whose first book focused on analyzing everyday interactional data generated in a college writing classroom, I had developed a transcription style largely based on conventions used in conversation analysis (Hepburn & Bolden, 2013) while omitting aural data that I could not independently verify through my careful listening (e.g., some auditory elements are entirely inaccessible to me, such as rising intonation or changes in pitch). I wanted to engage with the signed interviews using an interactional stance, which meant accounting for not only intricacies of how signs were produced (Kusters, Spotti, Swanwick, & Tapio, 2017; Valli, Lucas, Mulrooney, & Rankin, 2011), but also turn-taking and pauses (Power & Dal Martello, 1996; Sacks, Schegloff, & Jefferson, 1978), embodied movements (Kendon, 2004; Olinger, 2020), eye contact and gaze (Burke, 2014; Everts, 2004), manipulation of and attention to objects and artifacts in the material surround (Wolfe, 2005), and more. Unfortunately, I found that it was not possible for me to simply rely upon my familiar practices for transcribing and representing spoken interview data in working with the sign language interviews, and I found few models in the sign language studies research of analyses that paid close, fine-grained attention to sign language users' interactional moves in concert with one another.

I had assumed during data generation and conducting interviews that my lack of knowledge regarding how to transcribe sign language was merely an artifact of not being as familiar with sign language socio/linguistics as I should be. I further assumed that once I immersed myself in the sign language socio/linguistics literature, I would learn strategies and practices for transcription that would work for me. What I found instead is that there is no standard or widely used means for moving sign language, a spatiotemporal-visual language, into a written form. Researchers have developed numerous strategies such as: 1) relying on a transcription of an interpreter's voicing (e.g., Babcock, 2012); 2) glossing signs (using an English word in all-caps to represent a sign), sometimes accompanied by video stills and/ or access to video data (Winston & Roy, 2015); 3) phonetic transcription (e.g., the Stokoe system [Valli et al., 2011, pp. 28–33] and the Liddell and Johnson system [Valli et al., 2011, pp. 41–45]);[5] 4) reproducing video stills, usually combined with descriptions of the signs produced (e.g., Kusters, 2017); and 5) translating signed speech into a written language, usually with little to no attention to the linguistic or interactional elements of the signed conversation.[6] Each of these approaches offers different affordances and analytic possibilities, and selecting among them depends upon the research questions and the different goals of the researcher and participants. Unfortunately, none of these approaches were well-suited for supporting interactional analyses that could respond to the research questions I was asking about how disability emerged and was mutually identified by interviewer and interviewee.

I began working with the signed interviews by creating a rough transcript which would enable me, as I worked across the broader data set, to identify particular sections of these interviews for deeper analysis or more detailed transcription. I relied on a variety of strategies to generate these rough transcripts. Sometimes I translated ASL signs into English phrases and sentences while other times I drew on a combination of speechreading and signs called code-blending to produce what I interpreted as the speaker's intended utterance in English. I sometimes relied on glosses of specific signs, and sometimes I made notes to myself to describe particularities of the sign production that I noticed, as the interview participants and I all displayed varying degrees of ASL fluency and different degrees of reliance on "English-y" signing patterns. Let me give you an example. While I can understand ASL when produced by other people, and am experienced at working with sign language interpreters, I communicate largely in English using my voice during most of my daily life. This means that when I produce signs for particular terms or utterances, I sometimes rely on my knowledge of English glosses rather than on conceptually appropriate signs. In ASL there are different signs to communicate "call someone by their name" and "call someone on the telephone." Several times in the interview data I used the sign for "call someone on the telephone" when I intended to communicate "call someone by name." I described in my rough transcripts these conceptual inaccuracies, and where I noticed it, preliminary descriptions of my use of space. In ASL, the three-dimensional space around the signer is an important resource for conveying meaning. However, because I am not accustomed to including space in my language production, I tend to use a smaller, more limited signing space than do more experienced sign language users, making my signs sometimes difficult to follow.

Creating these rough transcripts was an important step in the analytic process, but they did not move the videorecorded interview data into a form that would enable detailed analysis, particularly since I was not systematic about noticing in these rough transcripts all of my conceptual inaccuracies or rigorously accounting for my own or interviewees' sign production, gaze, embodied movements, and use of artifacts. As an act of theory in which researchers select particular information to which they will attend (Bezemer & Mavers, 2011; Mishler, 1991; Ochs, 1979), transcription always involves balancing different priorities and making choices about how to represent embodied and linguistic actions in text. I understood my responsibility as one in which I needed to develop conventions for representing the different layers of interactional information I wanted to attend to analytically: how could I account for the way speakers' gaze behaviors shaped involvement? How could the transcripts illustrate the different signing styles and practices being used by interviewer and interviewee?[7] These questions about transcription are in some ways the inverse of the methodological point made earlier regarding uniform interviewing processes. In order to engage this sign language data alongside the spoken language data, I must ensure that my conclusions are not introduced by the ways that I document and transcribe that data.

In doing this work, I was also learning that it *is* indeed easier for me to navigate sign language interviews than spoken language interviews. But even though I can more easily navigate the video recordings, I am still – as I write this chapter – struggling with how to move that visual data into a written form suitable for the kind of close, detailed interactional linguistic analyses I regularly perform with spoken data. As Kusters et al. (2017) noted, while research strands in conversation analysis and ethnomethodology have taken up multimodal communicative resources such as eye gaze, embodied gestures and movements, and objects as part of communicative scenes, and while sign language-based research grounded in translingualism and multilingualism have acknowledged ways that sign language users move between visual, aural, and written modes, these two analytic approaches do not generally overlap with one another. The consequence is the dearth of interactional sign language research practices that I would have most benefited from and which I find myself now trying to generate nearly from scratch.

Challenge 2: How can researchers anonymize data or mask identifying details when analyzing a mode of communication that cannot be separated from the body?

In *Deafening Modernism*, literary theorist Sanchez (2015) argues for an understanding of language that inheres on the body, showing how ASL poetics can inform how we interpret the authorial bodies in and of modernist literature. Sanchez notes that ASL cannot be separated from the body, and further, that communication in ASL makes bodies dramatically visible to sighted audiences.[8] Both of these features complicate my analyses of the ASL interviews. While a relatively common means of analyzing participants' narratives could involve sharing brief interview clips or screenshots that capture key moments of interest, such methods also refuse participant anonymity. Sharing the interview videos would identify participants, and trying to re-represent or re-create participants' utterances (such as by signing them myself) would never replicate the linguistic and interactional elements I was most interested in analyzing from the interviews. And indeed, because signing styles are significantly inflected by race, gender, class, age, educational background, geographic region, and much more, any detailed representation of particular features of an interviewee's signing can run the risk of revealing their identity to others who are skilled at recognizing such linguistic nuances and cues. Attempts to describe signs in detail quickly become convoluted when trying to account for simultaneous communication or interaction. When writing for audiences who do not know ASL, handshape descriptors, movement, and more can be exceptionally difficult to describe. Consequently, decisions about how to record and transcribe the interview interactions must also take into account questions of how to represent and disseminate data in publications and other forms of knowledge generation.

In the absence of a method for representing in written form participants' interview accounts (De Fina, 2009), I found myself unable to move forward. I did not know how to work with what I was observing in a systematic way. I knew I needed to move from the rough transcripts that comprised different glosses, transliterations,[9] translations, observations about embodied movement, and notes to myself to an analysis that moved across this data and took seriously how these deaf academics narrated their experiences of disability in faculty life within the interview's interactional context. But if I could not systematically record these observations, how could I analyze across the data, much less publish findings from them?

Writing this chapter has been an effort to navigate what has felt like a paradox: my capacities as a tenured deaf white woman researcher who communicates using sign language enabled particular kinds of data generation and created some conditions for knowledge-building grounded in deaf academics' and communities' lived experiences (Burke & Nicodemus, 2013; Haualand, 2017; Robinson & Henner, 2017; Yabe, 2018) only to leave me somewhat stymied in working across the data and disseminating the kind of interactional research that I do.

Challenge 3: How can researchers create space for deaf participants and deaf researchers?

While it is beyond the scope of this chapter to offer specific how-to's given the complexity and range of deaf experiences and sign language use, I suggest that qualitative researchers who design projects that involve interviewing must critically examine the role and choice of interview modality and build opportunities for different means of interacting and communicating in to their research design. It is important for researchers and participants alike to ensure that they can navigate a communicative encounter responsibly, which means accounting for the researcher's as well as participants' access needs (see Haualand, 2017; Hou, 2017; Kerschbaum & Price, 2017; Kusters, 2012; Price & Kerschbaum, 2016). Such critical examination means conveying from the outset information about how interviews might be conducted as well as what choices might be available for those who volunteer for the study. It means identifying a way for participants to request accommodations and adjustments to the communicative scene, as well as building space into budgets for access and accommodation. Researchers must also consider how their analytic process might cut across different modes and types of interview interactions, which will likely require building familiarity with different communicative repertoires including instant messaging, text messaging, email, typing together in shared social space, and more.

But access is of course not just about communicative modality. It is about conditions for knowledge generation. This means attending to how deaf people access information about research as well as to how deaf academics receive material support for their scholarship and teaching and access to professional networks. It is about imagining access as part of every academic space and interaction. Right now, deaf people expend considerable energy asking for permission – over and over – to attend events, to be fully present in an interaction, to be part of academic environments that still assume that disability is absent unless and until it loudly announces itself. While deaf people have tremendous knowledge around how to create interactional access, this work cannot fall only on their shoulders. Too, access for deaf people is not only about deafness and sign language: identifications around race, ethnicity, gender, socioeconomic class, professional status, and more all inflect who participates and engages in scholarly research. The questions I am raising here about communicative modality for deaf people also open up possibilities for many others who do not rely on spoken language as their primary communicative mode. Learning to create space for deaf scholars and participants involves taking up what Minich (2016), in conversation with Schalk (2017) and Kim (2017), has called "disability studies as a methodology" (para. 5). For Minich, a disability studies methodology takes as a goal "*producing knowledge in support of justice* for people with stigmatized bodies and minds" (emphasis in original, para. 6). Such a methodology must engage in modes of knowledge production that involve – and center – those whose bodies and minds often lead them to be excluded or ignored.[10] Developing research processes that engage and include deaf participants can be an act of producing knowledge that supports inclusive practice, and it requires that deaf academics of all kinds take the lead in such research processes.[11]

Challenge 4: How should researchers navigate ethical challenges around relationships to participants, their use of sign language, and differential access to the conditions of knowledge production?

Up to this point I have been writing in such a way as to encourage readers of this chapter to include deaf participants and researchers in their work. But now I want to issue a warning: even as I am asking readers of this chapter to expand their research design and practice to be more inclusive, I must caution against a facile inclusion that does not take seriously the responsibilities involved in such engagement. Even for me, a researcher with proficiency in sign language communication, there remain significant minefields, and I have a great deal of work to do to ensure that my analyses are accountable and responsible to those who have shared their stories with me.

One such minefield, for instance, is that while I could work closely with the data to create an English translation of the signed interview conversation and accounts, those translations would not enable me to perform the kind of conversation analytic and linguistic analyses required for me to answer my questions about the interactional emergence and construction of disability. Another strategy could involve working closely with interviewees to generate a translation that they agree fits their interview utterances, but this option would ask even more of the interviewees' time in a way that would not be asked of interviewees who spoke aloud during their interviews.[12] Making such a request is further problematic when considering that deaf academics are not only exceptionally busy as faculty members, but are also doing double-duty efforts around securing access (see, e.g., Brueggemann & Kerschbaum, 2015; Burke, 2017; Burke & Nicodemus, 2013; Fink, Butler, Stremlau, Kerschbaum, & Brueggemann, 2020). Complicating matters even more, deaf academics often have other disability identifications, may be DeafBlind, and may have other marginalized identifications, such as being BIPOC, working class, first-generation, and/or multilingual (Bienvenu, 2008; Dunn, 2008; Erevelles & Kafer, 2010; Pearson, 2010; Rashid, 2010). All of these identifications matter to how deaf academics navigate dominant attitudes, orientations, and beliefs within predominantly white and predominantly hearing/non-disabled institutions, departments, and scholarly organizations. The response, then, to ensuring inclusion must focus on providing additional support rather than additional demands on deaf academics' time and energy.

These ethical questions also pertain to issues of community membership, insider and outsider status, and researchers' relationships to those communities. These are concerns for all researchers and not specific to this chapter, but I want to point to some particular issues that can come up for researchers working with signing deaf participants. That I am deaf myself, know sign language, and could conduct interviews in sign language likely led some participants to agree to participate in the project who might have chosen not to under different circumstances. For researchers who might need to work with a sign language interpreter to conduct an interview with a signing deaf person, there are significant issues around interpretation styles and practices that are important to take seriously. Burke (2017) offered an important overview of this, while asserting the importance for deaf people to have the option to choose their accommodations (see also Fink et al., 2020). Researchers who do not know sign language themselves run the risk of over-focusing on the interpreter's words and the interpreter's role in the communicative situation rather than the deaf participant's, and they face significant challenges in supporting the creation of communicative settings that facilitate interviewer and interviewee engagement. Even I, as someone who works with interpreters in all aspects of my professional life, is comfortable conversing in ASL (even with my imperfect signing skills), and feels her full body relax when surrounded by others communicating in sign language, struggled to account for sign language and embodied language production in my scholarly writing.

My access to communities of deaf academics as well as my signing skills might enable involvement and participation from those deaf academics in my research. But, as I've been showing throughout this chapter, that access does not mean that I will be able to move those interviews into the written forms I am most familiar with producing in my life as an academic, and it does not obviate me from my responsibility to hold myself accountable to those who gave of their time and resources to support my research. I am still figuring out what I am going to do with these data – even as I am *sure* I am going to do something with them. My goal in this work is to support the creation of inclusive academic environments and enhance practices of interactional accessibility.

Conclusions

In radical crip communities founded on principles of care described by Piepzna-Samarasinha (2018), an orientation to collective care works to move and support all members of a community. This often takes forms not readily described in a research methods section or anticipated when submitting an IRB. In designing an interview study founded on principles of an "interdependent disability studies methodology" (Price & Kerschbaum, 2016, p. 22), doing interviews with signing deaf people seemed an important way to move, and I had numerous competencies and resources that supported those moves. But I went into it naively, thinking that my communicative skills with ASL were most of what I needed and that I could figure everything else out as I went along. My hope is for this chapter to both support future researchers in engaging with signing deaf people across a wide set of communicative repertoires in their knowledge generation projects as well as to provide caution regarding the responsibilities we have as researchers to the people and communities we work with.

Notes

1 Robinson and Henner (2018), Smith and Andrews (2015), Woodcock, Rohan, and Campbell (2007).

2 While numbers are difficult to cite given the lack of available data, there are many educational and linguistic barriers faced by signing deaf people in academia, and signing deaf academics who do not communicate orally are underrepresented even at deaf colleges and universities.

3 It would be accurate to describe my signing as "English-y," as strongly influenced by rules governing English language production. I make less use of numerous language features developed within ASL, such as topicalization, use of three-dimensional space, and facial expressions than do more-fluent ASL speakers.

4 For more on this process, see Kerschbaum (2014, p. 22).

5 This strategy is most commonly used to analyze brief utterances and is not generally suitable for interactional analysis or legible outside of sign language linguistics.

6 Morgan (2005) provides a useful discussion of some of these transcription challenges as they pertain to sign language interaction.

7 Too, this question raises concerns about anonymity given the small number of signing deaf academics. Any accounting of a deaf academic's signing style risks identifying them, if not to mainstream audiences, then almost certainly within the very small world of deaf academics.

8 Natasha Abner (personal communication) noted that the lack of conventions for disembodiment in spoken languages further illustrates the point that the challenges around sign language transcription are in many ways related to conventions that have been readily developed for spoken language but not for signed languages.

9 While transliteration most often refers to an approach to sign language interpreting that works to maintain English structures and near-simultaneous language production according to a speaker's utterances, in this context I use it to mean moving ASL utterances into English while maintaining much of the signed utterance's sequencing and concepts.

10 It is important to acknowledge that this challenge is not limited to deaf academics. Abner noted on an earlier draft of this chapter that for pretty much any qualitative research topic, we generally do not know how that topic plays out among deaf people and many other people with disabilities because so few scholars have built accessibility into their research.

11 This is a central argument throughout Bauman and Murray (2014). Too, Robinson and Henner (2018) have critiqued the lack of representation of deaf professors and instructors in teaching ASL language courses, acknowledging the underrepresentation of deaf academics even in areas of study that most directly impact them.

12 For researchers working across languages, it is not uncommon to use community members as translators and research assistants, but in the case of deaf academics this remains sticky given the smallness of the deaf academic community and the role that confidentiality and/or anonymity may play for the data.

References

Babcock, R. D. (2012). *Tell me how it reads: Tutoring deaf and hearing students in the writing center*. Washington, DC: Gallaudet University Press.

Bauman, H. L., & Murray, J. J. (Eds.). (2014). *Deaf gain: Raising the stakes for human diversity*. Minneapolis, MN: University of Minnesota Press.

Bezemer, J., & Mavers, D. (2011). Multimodal transcription as academic practice: A social semiotic perspective. *International Journal of Social Research Methodology*, *14*(3), 191–206.

Bienvenu, M. J. (2008). Queer as deaf: Intersections. In H. L. Bauman (Ed.), *Open your eyes: Deaf studies talking* (pp. 264–273). Minneapolis, MN: University of Minnesota Press.

Brueggemann, B. J., & Kerschbaum, S. L. (2015). Disability: Representation, disclosure, access, and interdependence. In G. Colón-Semenza & G. A. Sullivan (Eds.), *How to build a life in the humanities* (pp. 183–192). New York: Palgrave.

Burke, T. B. (2014). Armchairs and stares: On the privation of deafness. In H. L. Bauman & J. J. Murray (Eds.), *Deaf gain: Raising the stakes for human diversity* (pp. 3–22). Minneapolis, MN: University of Minnesota Press.

Burke, T. B. (2017). Choosing accommodations: Signed language interpreting and the absence of choice. *Kennedy Institute for Ethics Journal*, *27*(2), 267–299.

Burke, T. B., & Nicodemus, B. (2013). Coming out of the hard of hearing closet: Reflections on a shared journey in academia. *Disability Studies Quarterly*, *33*(2). Retrieved from https://dsq-sds.org/article/view/3706/3239

De Fina, A. (2009). Narratives in interview: The case of accounts: For an interactional approach to narrative genres. *Narrative Inquiry*, *19*(2), 233–258.

Dunn, L. (2008). The burden of racism and audism. In H. L. Bauman (Ed.), *Open your eyes: Deaf studies talking* (pp. 235–250). Minneapolis, MN: University of Minnesota Press.

Erevelles, N., & Kafer, A. (2010). Committed critique: An interview with Nirmala Erevelles. In S. Burch & A. Kafer (Eds.), *Deaf and disability studies: Interdisciplinary perspectives* (pp. 204–21). Washington, DC: Gallaudet University Press.

Everts, E. (2004). Modalities of turn-taking in blind/sighted interaction: Better to be seen and not heard? In P. LeVine & R. Scollon (Eds.), *Discourse and technology: Multimodal discourse analysis* (pp. 128–145). Washington, DC: Georgetown University Press.

Fink, M., Butler, J., Stremlau, T., Kerschbaum, S. L., & Brueggemann, B. J. (2020). Honoring access needs at academic conferences through Computer Assisted Real-time Captioning (CART) and sign language interpreting. *College Composition and Communication*, *72*(1), 103–106.

Harmon, K. (2010). Deaf matters: Compulsory hearing and ability trouble. In S. Burch & A. Kafer (Eds.), *Deaf and disability studies: Interdisciplinary perspectives* (pp. 31–47). Washington, DC: Gallaudet University Press.

Haualand, H. (2017). When inclusion excludes. Deaf, researcher – Either, none, or both. In A. Kusters, M. De Meulder, & D. O'Brien (Eds.), *Innovations in deaf studies: The role of deaf scholars* (pp. 317–337). Oxford: Oxford University Press.

Hepburn, A., & Bolden, G. B. (2013). The conversation analytic approach to transcription. In J. Sidnell & T. Stivers (Eds.), *Handbook of conversation analysis* (pp. 57–76). Oxford: Wiley-Blackwell Publishing.

Hou, L. Y.-S. (2017). Negotiating language practices and language ideologies in fieldwork: A reflexive meta-documentation. In A. Kusters, M. De Meulder, & D. O'Brien. (Eds.), *Innovations in deaf studies: The role of deaf scholars* (pp. 339–359). Oxford: Oxford University Press.

Kendon, A. (2004). *Gesture: Visible action as utterance*. Cambridge: Cambridge University Press.

Kerschbaum, S. L. (2014). *Toward a new rhetoric of difference*. Urbana, IL: NCTE.

Kerschbaum, S. L., & Price, M. (2017). Centering disability in qualitative interviewing. *Research in the Teaching of English, 52*(1), 98–107.

Kim, J. B. (2017). Toward a crip-of-color critique: Thinking with Minich's "Enabling whom?". *Lateral, 6*(1). Retrieved August 21, 2020, from http://csalat eral.org/issue/6-1/forum-alt-humanities-critical-disability-studies-crip-of-color-critique-kim/

Kusters, A. (2012). Being a deaf white anthropologist in Adamorobe: Some ethical and methodological issues. In U. Zeshan & C. de Vos (Eds.), *Sign languages in village communities: Anthropological and linguistic insights* (pp. 27–52). Boston, MA: De Gruyter Mouton.

Kusters, A. (2017). "Our hands must be connected": Visible gestures, tactile gestures and objects in interactions featuring a deafblind customer in Mumbai. *Social Semiotics, 27*(4), 394–410.

Kusters, A., Spotti, M., Swanwick, R., & Tapio, E. (2017). Beyond languages, beyond modalities: Transforming the study of semiotic repertoires. *International Journal of Multilingualism, 14*(3), 219–232.

Minich, J. A. (2016). Enabling whom? Critical disability studies now. *Lateral, 5*(1). Retrieved August 21, 2020, from http://csalateral.org/issue/5-1/forum-alt-humanities-critical-disability-studies-now-minich/

Mishler, E. (1991). Representing discourse: The rhetoric of transcription. *Journal of Narrative and Life History, 1*(4), 255–280.

Morgan, G. (2005). Transcription of child sign language: A focus on narrative. *Sign Language and Linguistics, 8*(1–2), 117–128.

Ochs, E. (1979). Transcription as theory. *Developmental Pragmatics, 10*(1), 43–72.

Olinger, A. (2020). Visual embodied actions in interview-based writing research: A methodological argument for video. *Written Communication, 37*(2), 167–207.

Pearson, H. (2010). Complicating intersectionality through the identities of a hard of hearing Korean adoptee: An autoethnography. *Equity and Excellence in Education, 43*(3), 341–356.

Piepzna-Samarasinha, L. L. (2018). *Care work: Dreaming disability justice*. Vancouver, BC: Arsenal Pulp Press.

Power, R. J. D., & Dal Martello, M. F. (1996). Some criticisms of Sacks, Schegloff, and Jefferson on turn-taking. *Semiotica, 58*(1/2), 29–40.

Price, M., & Kerschbaum, S. L. (2016). Stories of methodology: Interviewing sideways, crooked, and crip. *The Canadian Journal of Disability Studies, 5*(3), 18–56.

Rashid, K. (2010). Intersecting reflections. In S. Burch & A. Kafer (Eds.), *Deaf and disability studies: Interdisciplinary perspectives* (pp. 22–30). Washington, DC: Gallaudet University Press.

Robinson, O. E., & Henner, J. (2017). The personal is political in *The Deaf Mute Howls*: Deaf epistemology seeks disability justice. *Disability and Society, 32*(9), 1416–1436.

Robinson, O. E., & Henner, J. (2018). Authentic voices, authentic encounters: Cripping the university through American Sign Language. *Disability Studies*

Quarterly, 38(4). Retrieved August 21, 2020, from https://dsq-sds.org/article/view/6111/5128

Sacks, H., Schegloff, E., & Jefferson, G. (1978). A simplest systematics for the organization of turn-taking for conversation. In J. Schenkein (Ed.), *Studies in the organization of conversational interaction* (pp. 7–55). New York: Academic Press.

Sanchez, R. (2015). *Deafening modernism: Embodied language and visual poetics in American literature*. New York: New York University Press.

Schalk, S. (2017). Critical disability studies as methodology. *Lateral, 6*(1). Retrieved August 21, 2020, from http://csalateral.org/issue/6-1/forum-alt-humanities-critical-disability-studies-methodology-schalk/

Smith, D. H., & Andrews, J. F. (2015). Deaf and hard of hearing faculty in higher education: Enhancing access, equity, policy, and practice. *Disability and Society, 30*(10), 1521–1536.

Valli, C., Lucas, C., Mulrooney, K. J., & Rankin, M. N. P. (2011). *Linguistics of American Sign Language: An introduction* (5th ed.). Washington, DC: Gallaudet University Press.

Winston, E. A., & Roy, C. (2015). Discourse analysis and sign languages. In A. C. Schembri & C. Lucas (Eds.), *Sociolinguistics and deaf communities* (pp. 95–119). Cambridge: Cambridge University Press.

Wolfe, J. (2005). Gesture and collaborative planning: A case study of a student writing group. *Written Communication, 22*(3), 298–332.

Woodcock, K., Rohan, M. J., & Campbell, L. (2007). Equitable representation of deaf people in mainstream academia: Why not? *Higher Education, 53,* 359–379. https://doi.org/10.1007/s10734-005-2428-x

Yabe, M. (2018). The journey of a deaf translingual tutor. *Writing on the Edge: On Writing and Teaching Writing, 28*(2), 73–85.

6 Inside/out

Qualitative methods, online archives, and advocacy

Alice Wong

Introduction

This is an atypical book chapter in a textbook on qualitative research. Rather than an introduction in which I produce a litany of pertinent work on the topics covered in this chapter, I will produce a series of caveats.

- I am not an archivist nor do I have a degree in archival or disability studies.
- I write about my activism and use the terms 'archive' and 'online archives' with an informal understanding of them. For example, I do not use metadata or have any protocols on identifying, locating, and interpreting records.
- I explicitly write in plain language and do not have institutional access to libraries and online journals. Rather than asking university-based friends to send me PDFs, I use the tools available to me: Google and scholars I know personally to situate this chapter within various literatures.

Archives and archivists have never been neutral. Gracen M. Brilmyer (2018), a disabled PhD student in information studies at the University of California, Los Angeles (UCLA), writes:

> Disability studies provides critical models that recognize history, conceptualize oppression, and can expand the ways in which records are produced, processed, and understood (p. 96). . . . There is inherent power in the creation of records, the formation of archives, and the ways in which archival material is described and processed. Feminist disability studies opens up archival processes as sites for contestation and exposes the layers of power within an archives. A connection to disability, through a political/relational archival approach, first

provides an immediate politicization of archival processes by surfacing the power of language as well as how archives have been historically used against disabled people.

(p. 102)

Brilmyer's research (Caswell, Gabiola, Zavala, Brilmyer, & Cifor, 2018; Brilmyer, Gabiola, Zavala, & Caswell, 2019) lies at the intersection of disability studies, sexuality studies, and archival studies and offers important context to this chapter. However, I must be honest and admit I do not have the capacity or proficiency to fully situate this chapter in their body of work. I believe Brilmyer's emergent research is incredibly exciting and necessary and should be required reading for anyone interested in disabled people, their experiences, and relationships in both digital and physical archives.

Part personal essay and show and tell, I invite you to meet me where I am and imagine where I place within the literature.

Academic insider/outsider

I loved social studies and English in high school, and in my senior year I took a sociology class that opened my eyes at how to see the world. As an undergraduate I double majored in English and sociology at Indiana University-Indianapolis. During my years there I had some sociologists who mentored me and gave me opportunities as a research and teaching assistant. Dr. Linda Haas hired me as a student mentor to a one-credit class for new non-traditional students on some of the basics of being a student such as learning how to email and use the library. Dr. Carol Gardner (1995), a student of Erving Goffman, introduced me to *Stigma* (1963) and *The Presentation of Self in Everyday Life* (1959) that resonated deeply with my own lived experience as a disabled person. Dr. Gardner hired me as a research assistant and I learned grounded theory and content analysis for the first time. Imagine my delight discovering a disabled activist/sociologist, Irving K. Zola (2003), and his work in medical sociology and disability studies.

As a disabled student who was the first to go to college in her family in the early 1990s, I was hungry to learn and escape the confines of what the world thought I was 'good enough' for. My experiences commuting from my suburban home to and from the downtown campus were difficult – because I lived north of the county line, I was ineligible for paratransit. Rather, Vocational Rehabilitation paid for a paramedic service to take me to school twice a week. How medical model can you get? Accessible transport via ambulance! I held my urine and didn't eat or drink much during days I spent 6–8 hours on campus even though I had one bathroom break with a personal assistant. The first few years were a lonely and challenging existence. The relationships I had with faculty members like Dr. Gardner, Dr. Haas, and Dr. David W. Moller kept my spirits alive because they believed in my potential and encouraged my growth. Their friendship and generosity gave me hope that I might have a future in academia.

I could not imagine exactly what my professional future would look like because I didn't know of any disabled academic role models or fellow disabled students interested in research. What I did know was that I enjoyed qualitative research – interviewing people, poring through transcripts, coding, analyzing, and writing. Learning more about disability studies, I wanted to produce more research about disability by actual disabled scholars. This was going to be my niche. Thanks to a referral from Dr. Gardner, I called the late Dr. Paul K. Longmore (2003) out of the blue one night as I was debating whether to apply for graduate school in San Francisco. I must have sounded like an insecure crip, calling Paul and asking him what the disability community was like in the SF Bay Area. I asked him, "Do you think I could do this, move to San Francisco, attend school, and find my people?" Even though we were strangers, Paul treated me like a friend and gave an emphatic "YES. You can do this."

In 1997 I made the westward trek and never looked back. I felt certain that my professional future would involve a life in the academy researching, writing, or teaching. Little did I know I was about to hit a brick wall filled with anxiety, insecurity, and self-doubt that changed the trajectory of my life.

San Francisco felt like home the minute I arrived at University of California San Francisco's (UCSF) Parnassus campus. I met Paul and other disabled scholars such as the late great Barbara Faye Waxman Fiduccia (1994), who became my role model since I also wanted to do research on disabled women and reproductive health. I slowly started becoming involved with the Bay Area disability community and attended annual meetings of the Society for Disability Studies where I met other graduate students and scholars doing some amazing work.

At the same time I struggled as a first year graduate student. My small cohort was intimidating. Other than myself and one other student, all of them had multiple degrees or came from other careers. I quickly discovered how out of depth I was in sociology theory and quantitative methods. My only saving grace was qualitative methods with Dr. Adele Clarke (2005), who also served as my advisor. I took to grounded theory and standpoint theory reading works by Glaser and Strauss (1967) and Dorothy Smith (1989). For this course I interviewed several disabled women about the work of creating access to reproductive and sexual health care. It was a joy recruiting and interviewing these women and creating theory by coding through their transcripts. Swimming in codes upon codes, ideas upon ideas, was invigorating. I felt in my element.

By my second year I knew something was seriously wrong with my progress. I was unable to keep up with the assignments and readings. I began to take numerous extensions and did not do well in my qualifying exams. Everything became overwhelming and exhausting – my bodymind did not cooperate with me anymore. It forced me to slow down and listen to it. Years of being driven to excel and become 'independent' and navigating ableist microaggressions and inaccessible environments led me to a limbo where I did not have the capacity to complete my work. I was full of shame and did not see a path forward. Faculty members were understanding up to a point but after several years of delay Dr. Clarke shared her concerns and insisted on creating a plan for me to complete my outstanding coursework with a specific timeline or else. While I was able to buckle down and complete everything, I knew that I wasn't ready to move forward toward the dissertation phase.

I made the mistake of thinking I had to have a PhD in order to conduct qualitative research. Once I figured that out, I switched gears to life as a staff research associate after receiving what is considered a 'terminal' Master's degree since my program was PhD track only. Having a realistic view of the stress and struggle graduate students faced during and after their dissertations (especially the pressures of publishing and job searches) gave me a clear sense that my health and wellness would be at risk. Letting go of the idea of being a full professor was a blow to my ego but one of the best damn decisions I ever made.

In 2019 Christine Marshall, a queer deaf activist and student at the University of California at Santa Cruz, created a hashtag on Twitter: #WhyDisabledPeopleDropOut (Sadeque, 2019). Many people started to share their stories. It brought back painful memories and I decided to share mine as well. Here are a few excerpts:

I was inside and part of a campus community for many years until I needed more. Being an outsider has afforded me greater access and freedom to write and work the way I want, even though it's without institutional support. Even writing this chapter I have qualms about how it will be received since it's not chock full of citations or supported by an extensive literature review.

Working on various research projects over ten years at UCSF gave me the opportunity to do hands-on qualitative research: focus groups, interviews, surveys, etc. Looking back, all of these experiences prepared me for my life as a community activist/scholar.

Alice Wong ☑
@SFdirewolf

Really appreciating everyone's powerful stories with the #WhyDisabledPeopleDropout tag.

Here's my not-so-brief story.

I loved sociology ever since high school and knew the humanities & social sciences was my jam. [thread]

5:58 AM · Apr 24, 2019 · Twitter for iPhone

Figure 6.1 Screenshot of a Tweet from April 24, 2019, 5:58 am by @ SFdirewolf: Really appreciating everyone's powerful stories with the #WhyDisabledPeopleDropout tag. Here's my not-so-brief story. I loved sociology ever since high school and knew the humanities & social sciences was my jam. [thread]

Sharing (and documenting) is caring

The beginning of my second life as an academic outsider began when I created the Disability Visibility Project (DVP) in 2014, partnering with StoryCorps to record oral histories and archive them at the Library of Congress. I originally planned the partnership as a one-year campaign, a way for disabled people to celebrate and preserve their stories, histories of us and by us. What started as a small oral history project kept going and blew up into a movement. The DVP now has more than 140 oral histories, the largest and longest community partnership StoryCorps ever had which resulted in a small but mighty archive of the disability zeitgeist. And the project has expanded into an online community that creates, shares, and amplifies disability media and culture through podcasts, articles, Twitter chats, and more.

After several years of working on the DVP in addition to my day job as a staff research associate, I felt the pull to change up my life. The DVP was and continues to be a one-person operation financed early on by my income and I made the decision to devote to it full time in the third or fourth year of its existence. I became an independent research consultant as part of my side-hustle and launched a Patreon campaign to help crowdfund the costs involved with my advocacy and media making. I had no blueprint or

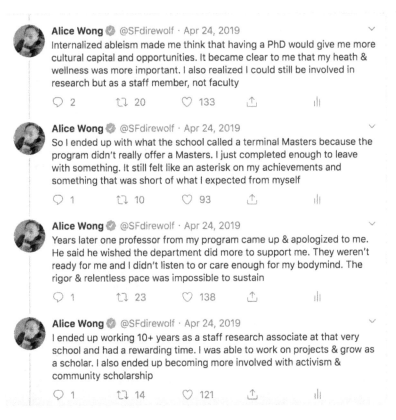

Figure 6.2 Screenshot of four Tweets from April 24, 2019 by @SFdirewolf:

Internalized ableism made me think that having a PhD would give me more cultural capital and opportunities. It became clear to me that my heath & wellness was more important. I also realized I could still be involved in research but as a staff member, not faculty

So I ended up with what the school called a terminal Masters because the program didn't really offer a Masters. I just completed enough to leave with something. It still felt like an asterisk on my achievements and something that was short of what I expected from myself

Years later one professor from my program came up & apologized to me. He said he wished the department did more to support me. They weren't ready for me and I didn't listen to or care enough for my bodymind. The rigor & relentless pace was impossible to sustain

I ended up working 10+ years as a staff research associate at that very school and had a rewarding time. I was able to work on projects & grow as a scholar. I also ended up becoming more involved with activism & community scholarship

Alice Wong ✔ @SFdirewolf · Apr 24, 2019
I don't regret my decision to drop out. It was an act of liberation and led me to where I am today which is exactly what I was meant to be.

But my memories of the pain, the loneliness, the insecurity, the anxiety, and lack of support still haunts me.

◯ 5   ↱ 25   ♡ 195   ⬆   ⅲ

Alice Wong ✔ @SFdirewolf · Apr 24, 2019
Every once in a while I wonder what I could have offered to the academy, what my contributions would have been to the fields of disability studies & medical sociology. It would have been epic, but that's their loss and we'll never know.

So ends my #WhyDisabledPeopleDropout story

◯ 15   ↱ 44   ♡ 274   ⬆   ⅲ

Figure 6.3 Screenshot of two Tweets from April 24, 2019 by @SFdirewolf:

I don't regret my decision to drop out. It was an act of liberation and led me to where I am today which is exactly what I was meant to be.

But my memories of the pain, the loneliness, the insecurity, the anxiety, and lack of support still haunts me.

Every once in a while I wonder what I could have offered to the academy, what my contributions would have been to the fields of disability studies & medical sociology. It would have been epic, but that's their loss and we'll never know.

So ends my #WhyDisabledPeopleDropout story

grand five-year plan. I knew that I wanted to keep creating and amplifying the work of disabled people through collaborations and deep relationships with multiple communities. And I wanted control and autonomy on how I do my work and goals I set for myself. The last few years has been quite an adventure in my activities and approaches to documenting and archiving the culture.

One of my joys in conducting qualitative research is asking good questions and learning from others. This joy transformed into a commitment and drive to share these stories online in as many different and accessible ways as possible. Unlike academics who publish their latest findings in a journal and primarily attend professional conferences, I want my work to be free and open without paywalls or the need for institutional access.

It is not enough to document and create new knowledge – we must be creative in getting disability culture and wisdom (and other valuable forms of qualitative research about all communities) out there in as many formats and platforms as possible. I am heartened to see so many academics blog, Tweet, and engage as scholars in various public spaces, both online and in person. I hope to see more of this as a way to bridge the divide between the 'Academy' and the 'Community' (which is a false binary to begin with).

Qualitative research in the field

Here are a few examples of my work as an activist, research consultant, and media maker which all rely on skills I learned from sociology: 1) oral histories for the DVP; 2) #GetWokeADA26, a paper co-authored by Villisa Thompson of RampYourVoice.com and me; 3) usage of Wakelet and other apps to curate the latest emergent online conversations centered on disability; and 4) hosting, interviewing, and audio producing the Disability Visibility podcast.

Oral histories

Through a license agreement with StoryCorps, I have access to all of the oral histories created for the DVP. Per their requirements, I can only publish short excerpts versus the entire interview. On my website over the years I have been slowly editing and uploading clips from the 140+ oral histories. Each blog post includes the audio link, text transcript, image, and image description. Each audio link is uploaded to Soundcloud which is another platform where people can discover and listen to these stories. I can also create playlists on Soundcloud based on topic at a later time to provide thematic groupings of these oral histories.

#GetWokeADA26 report

One reason I started the DVP came out of frustration about the lack of disability history and representation in mainstream media. The second reason was/is the overwhelming whiteness of what is considered the lived disability experience by society. I wanted more people, especially within the disability community, to understand the perspectives of disabled people of color as they are shaped by multiple axes of oppression including ableism. For the 26th anniversary of the ADA, I partnered with Vilissa Thompson, consultant, writer, social worker, and creator of the #DisabilityTooWhite hashtag. We created an online survey and asked disabled people of color to reflect on what the ADA and disability rights means to them. The title of our report (Thompson & Wong, 2016a, 2016b) was #GetWokeADA26 which also doubled as a hashtag online to create conversations along with the report. We also utilized the work of a disabled artist, Mike Mort, for our graphic.

DISABILITY VISIBILITY PROJECT | DVP INTERVIEW: ING WONG-WARD AND ALICE WONG

CATEGORIES
DVP Interviews,
Uncategorized

TAGS
Ableism, Canada, Disabled
journalists, Disabled Parents,
Families, journalism, Media
representation, Parenting,
Parents, pregnancy,
reproduction, Sex education,
Toronto

Alice Wong interviewed Ing Wong-Ward for the Disability Visibility
Project® at StoryCorps San Francisco on August 25, 2016. Ing shares with
Alice how she became a journalist and a disabled parent. Ing also talks
about her family and her daughter Zhenmei.

Figure 6.4 Screenshot from Disability Visibility Project featuring a DVP interview
between Ing Wong-Ward and Alice Wong. Text reads: Alice Wong
interviewed Ing Wong-Ward for the Disability Visibility Project® at
StoryCorps San Francisco on August 25, 2016. Ing shares with Alice
how she became a journalist and a disabled parent. Ing also talks about
her family and her daughter Zhenmei. Below is a Soundcloud audio link
featuring a photo of Ing and Alice. On the left is Ing Wong-Ward, a
Chinese Canadian disabled woman with short black hair and a cream top
with black decorative print on the sleeves. She is in a wheelchair with
a belt across her chest. On the right is Alice Wong, a Chinese American
disabled woman with short black hair and a black shirt with small white
cat paw prints. She is in a wheelchair and wearing a mask over her nose
attached to a tube for her ventilator.

The response yielded rich insights and tensions on life as disabled people
of color in the United States. In the two weeks we launched the survey,
50 individuals representing various people of color communities, disability
types, ages, and sexual identities and orientations answered our request to
share. The online survey covered the following topics:

- Impact of the ADA on disabled POC
- Intersectionality and disability rights
- Disability issues most pressing to disabled POC
- Perspectives on racism, diversity, ableism, and inequality within the
  disability community
- Recommendations: Partnership and collaboration with disabled POC

#GetWokeADA26
Disabled People of Color Speak Out

Part One

Vilissa Thompson
and
Alice Wong

Image: Mike Mort
@MikeeMort

Figure 6.5 White background with black text that reads: #GetWokeADA26 Disabled People of Color Speak Out, Part One. Vilissa Thompson and Alice Wong. On the left-hand side is an image of a Black Wonder Woman character in a wheelchair. She has rainbow wristbands and a golden lasso by her wheel. Image: Mike Mort @MikeeMort. On the lower right-hand side: Full report: RampYourVoice.com DisabilityVisibilityProject.com

The data we collected was extraordinary. Our report provided a thematic summary published in two parts, on Vilissa's website and the DVP for maximum reach.

We created graphics with selected powerful quotes from respondents and Tweeted them with the #GetWokeADA26 hashtag during July 2016 to add to the overall conversation about the ADA and disability rights.

This report does not show up in any social science databases or may not be cited by many disability studies scholars, but I find satisfaction that Vilissa and I produced qualitative research that deserved attention and visibility.

Archiving conversations from the disability twitterverse

Inaccessibility of websites and apps (Glaser, 2019) and the digital divide (Anderson & Perrin, 2007) continue to impact disabled people, disenfranchising them of the right to participate and access information. Speaking for myself, who has privilege in being able to afford broadband services, a laptop, a smartphone, and opportunities to learn how to

#GetWokeADA26

"...being Black, female, disabled and over 50 means I get less quality health care, hostile health care, and fewer opportunity for employment."

—Anonymous

Image: Mike Mort
@MikeeMort

**Full Report:
RampYourVoice.com
DisabilityVisibilityProject.com**

Figure 6.6 White background with black text that reads: #GetWokeADA26 ". . . being Black, female, disabled and over 50 means I get less quality health care, hostile health care, and fewer opportunity for employment." – Anonymous. On the left-hand side is an image of a Black Wonder Woman character in a wheelchair. She has rainbow wristbands and a golden lasso by her wheel. Image: Mike Mort @MikeeMort. On the lower right-hand side: Full report: RampYourVoice.com DisabilityVisibilityProject.com

use them, there's no doubt that the Internet has been a game changer. It allows me to work from home and participate in events through video-conferencing and other means.

I've become more 'alive' and active in online spaces where I can find and create community and become engaged with advocacy that works with my bodymind. Getting older means getting wiser on how I want to use my time, and digital access gave me the keys to build my own platform and maximize the dissemination of my work and other deep thoughts.

There is a constant creation and co-creation of stories, culture, information, and ideas on social media by marginalized people such as disabled people, especially multiply marginalized disabled people of color. Without a filter or gatekeeper, marginalized communities have direct access to public dialogue and a forum connecting with people. While this visibility can be beneficial, (e.g., raising a person's profile, eliciting opportunities, holding organizations and institutions accountable, and bringing attention to critical issues) the high risk of harassment, microaggressions, and toxicity

Disabled People of Color Highlighted in
#GetWokeADA26 Survey
colorwebmag.com/2016/08/03/dis...

#GetWokeADA26

"I am black.
I am a woman.
I am disabled.
I am magic."
—Joi Meyer Brewer

Full Report:
RampYourVoice.com
DisabilityVisibilityProject.com

Image: Mike Mort
@MikeeMort

6:00 AM · Aug 3, 2016 · WordPress.com

Figure 6.7 Screenshot of a Tweet by @Colorwebmag on August 3, 2016, 6:00 am
with the text:

Disabled People of Color Highlighted in #GetWokeADA26 Survey http://color
webmag.com/2016/08/03/dis . . . The Tweet includes an image with a white
background with black text that reads: #GetWokeADA26 "I am black. I am a woman.
I am disabled. I am magic." – Joi Meyer Brewer. On the left-hand side is an image
of a Black Wonder Woman character in a wheelchair. She has rainbow wristbands
and a golden lasso by her wheel. Image: Mike Mort @MikeeMort. On the lower
right-hand side: Full report: RampYourVoice.com DisabilityVisibilityProject.com

from these spaces can chip away at a person's space in online environments
(Anti-Defamation League, 2020).

It is a delicate balancing act for myself as I dwell in the very tensions that
keep me involved and away from Twitter. One reason why I stay is the rich,

nuanced, and complex conversations that occur simultaneously by disabled people around the world on the latest, most pressing issues. I retweet opinions and thoughts that I find interesting and worth sharing.

My activism with the DVP includes the organizing and moderating Twitter chats through partnerships such as #CripTheVote, a nonpartisan online movement encouraging the political participation of disabled people with Gregg Beratan and Andrew Pulrang. After every Twitter chat I would archive the one-hour conversation by using an application called Wakelet that allows you to find and save Tweets by hashtag or user. When a particular Twitter chat has a high number of participants and level of engagement, a single recap could include hundreds of Tweets. I put a lot of time, labor, and care in each recap. After pulling hundreds of Tweets and having them listed in chronological order, I review the entire collection deleting trolls, spam, or non-relevant content caught up in the search. I am careful to describe these recaps as a sample of the conversation since they are neither complete nor definitive. It is a sampling based on a particular time and search and my editing of the best ones.

Wakelet allows users to curate all kinds of content: text, video, Tweets, images, and links. I can combine different types of media all together and share them using a single URL. These collections become part of my page on the app where anyone can see, use, or share my public collection. One can also export these collections as PDFs and embed them in a website

Figure 6.8 Screenshot of Alice Wong's Wakelet account, @AliceWong9697 that has 49 followers, 195 collections, 25,000 bookmarks, and two group collections. There are three squares from left to right: a plus sign that says "Create a new collection," a collection "#Coronavirus and the disability community . . ." with 598 items, and "#CripTheVote live tweets the 2/25 . . ." The center square features a photo of a pair of hands washing with soap over a kitchen sink with fruit in the background on a white countertop. The right square has a plain black graphic with #CripTheVote in white.

allowing even more options to disseminate. Originally, I used an app called Storify when I started splashing around on Twitter and the danger of using any app is the possibility of it shutting down (which it did). Fortunately, there was a small window of time that allowed users to import their collections to Wakelet, an alternative that's now my go-to for archiving online content.

Why archive disability culture and wisdom?

From 2015 to March 2020, I created 195 collections in Storify and Wakelet comprising 25,000 pieces of content. All of this is data. Similar to the saying by Nora Ephron's mother, "Everything is copy," (Garber, 2016) I believe everything is data and it's up to all of us to document and archive them with care for future generations.

The reasons why I care (and share) often go back to the mission of the Disability Visibility Project which is "dedicated to creating, sharing, and amplifying disability media and culture." Our stories are not told enough, and too often they are from a non-disabled lens. Our stories and wisdom are not valued by a society that does not recognize us as a community with distinct histories and cultures. I see an incredible amount of wisdom and narratives created by disabled people online in the spirit of generosity AND in response to ableism and other forms of oppression.

The curious cat in me, shaped by my background in qualitative research, led me to interview disabled people on my website and podcast, Disability Visibility. Started in 2017, the podcast, available in multiple platforms such as iTunes, Spotify, and Google Play, features 72 episodes as of March 9, 2020. These episodes, all available on my website with audio and text transcripts, are another archive of disability culture and wisdom rooted in the past and present with an eye toward the future.

The conversations I am able to have with other disabled people are a precious gift. All of us can forget how significant they are until it's too late. Because these conversations can be ephemeral and scattered, curating them on Wakelet, a blog, or podcast is a way to preserve and make available our wisdom and culture to the public.

In a final example, during the writing of this book chapter (early March 2020) the coronavirus began to spread in the United States with increasingly alarming news and inadequate action by the federal government. Whenever there are emergencies or crises, marginalized communities know best how to survive because they are also the ones most adversely and disproportionately impacted. I began to retweet many chronically ill, immunocompromised, disabled, and homebound people who began to share their stories on how the coronavirus will affect them. Disabled people responded

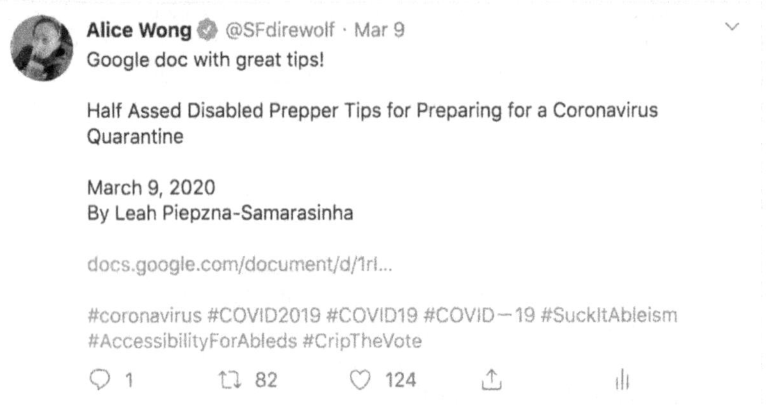
Alice Wong @SFdirewolf · Mar 9
Google doc with great tips!
Half Assed Disabled Prepper Tips for Preparing for a Coronavirus Quarantine
March 9, 2020
By Leah Piepzna-Samarasinha
docs.google.com/document/d/1rI...
#coronavirus #COVID2019 #COVID19 #COVID−19 #SuckItAbleism #AccessibilityForAbleds #CripTheVote
1
82
124

Figure 6.9 Screenshot of a Tweet by @SFdirewolf on March 9, 10:27 pm: Google doc with great tips! Half Assed Disabled Prepper Tips for Preparing for a Coronavirus Quarantine, March 9, 2020,By Leah Piepzna-Samarasinha https://docs.google.com/document/d/1rI . . .#coronavirus #COVID2019 #COVID19 #COVID–19 #SuckItAbleism #AccessibilityForAbleds #CripTheVote

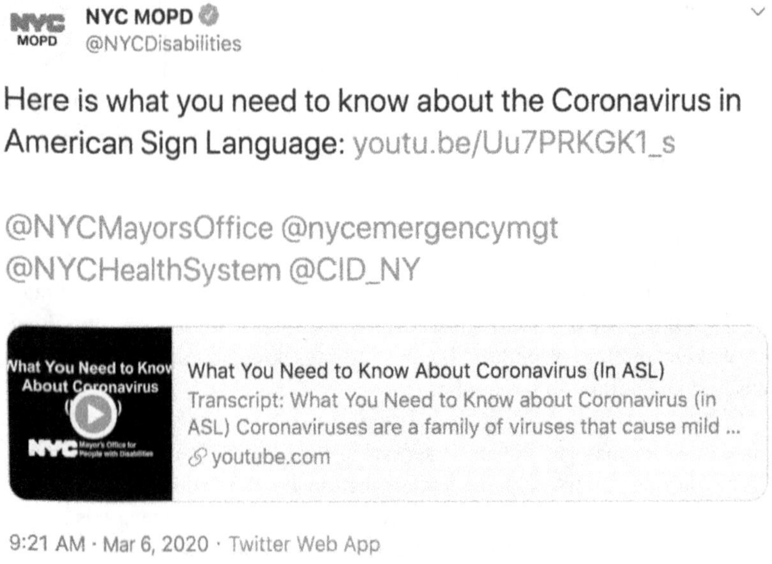
NYC MOPD
@NYCDisabilities
Here is what you need to know about the Coronavirus in American Sign Language: youtu.be/Uu7PRKGK1_s
@NYCMayorsOffice @nycemergencymgt @NYCHealthSystem @CID_NY
What You Need to Know About Coronavirus (In ASL)
Transcript: What You Need to Know about Coronavirus (in ASL) Coronaviruses are a family of viruses that cause mild ...
youtube.com
9:21 AM · Mar 6, 2020 · Twitter Web App

Figure 6.10 Screenshot of a Tweet by @NYCDisabilities on March 6, 9:21 am: Here is what you need to know about the Coronavirus in American Sign Language: https://youtu.be/Uu7PRKGK1_s @NYCMayorsOffice @nycemergencymgt @NYCHealthSystem @CID_NY

Dawn M Gibson
@DawnMGibson

This one goes out to all of our people. It's okay to say that #COVID19 or other threats have you worried for your future.

It's okay to do what you have to manage your risk. #Disability

> **Dawn M Gibson** @DawnMGibson · Mar 5
> My latest: I Still Have Complications from the 2009 Swine Flu, So Understand Why #COVID19 Is Worrying People with 'Underlying Health Conditions': creakyjoints.org/living-with-ar... #SpoonieChat #LupusChat #Disability
> Show this thread

10:02 AM · Mar 5, 2020 · Twitter Web App

Figure 6.11 Screenshot of a quote Tweet by @DawnMGibson on March 5, 2020, 10:02 am: This one goes out to all of our people. It's okay to say that #COVID19 or other threats have you worried for your future. It's okay to do what you have to manage your risk. #Disability. Below is another Tweet by Dawn: My latest: I Still Have Complications from the 2009 Swine Flu, So Understand Why #COVID19 Is Worrying People with 'Underlying Health Conditions': https://creakyjoints.org/living-with-ar/. . . #SpoonieChat #LupusChat #Disability

to the hoarding of medical supplies and hand sanitizers, recommendations on social distancing and stockpiling medications, and media coverage on who is most 'vulnerable.'

Using Wakelet, I started to search through my timeline for retweets from the disability community. Within 4–5 days disabled people were organizing mutual aid, hosting Twitter chats, and writing articles about the coronavirus. I wanted to collect information that could be used as a resource as well as stories highlighting questions and perspectives missed by the media. Each day I came across more data that provided a snapshot of this historic moment in the United States. This collection currently has 598 pieces of content and will likely grow as the pandemic develops. Not only are these online archives material for use by researchers, they are for us by us in acknowledgment of our intellectual and emotional labor. I love what I do and this particular example is done out of a sense of urgency and need.

Conclusions

Firmly and happily situated outside of the academy and in dialogue with you, Dear Reader, I have some final thoughts and questions on how qualitative researchers can and should work with disabled activists and community scholars.

- What are the ways you are making your research accessible and open to broader audiences?
- If you use social media, do you follow and learn from organizers, activists, and creators from the communities you are studying?
- How are you uplifting and amplifying the scholarship of people outside of the academy, such as inviting them to speak at your classes, being on a panel, co-presenting at meetings, and co-authoring and designing research projects and papers?
- How many non-academic scholars do you cite and if you can't name any, why not?
- If you are conducting research about a marginalized community, how will you solicit feedback and critique from people with lived experience?
- Before diving into research about a marginalized community ask yourself if you are the best person to do this and whether it's appropriate to partner or refer others who have been doing the work.

Here is some advice based on my own experiences.

- DO pay disabled people for their time, advice, and feedback.
- DON'T use a disabled person's hashtag, quotes, images, concepts, or content without attribution or permission.
- DO get involved with your local disability community or online spaces to broaden your understanding.
- DO support the work of organizers, activists, and disabled creators (sharing their links and fundraisers, buying their work, hiring them).
- DON'T judge the quality of a person's research or scholarship by the way they write or how fast/slow/differently they write, communicate, think, or move.

References

(2018, December 1). *DVP interview: Ing Wong-Ward and Alice Wong*. Disability Visibility Project. Retrieved from https://disabilityvisibilityproject.com/2018/12/01/dvp-interview-ing-wong-ward-and-alice-wong/

Anderson, M., & Perrin, A. (2017, April 7). Disabled Americans are less likely to use technology. *Pew Research Center*. Retrieved from www.pewresearch.org/fact-tank/2017/04/07/disabled-americans-are-less-likely-to-use-technology/

Anti-Defamation League. (2020, June). *Online hate and harassment: The American experience 2020*. Center for Technology and Society. Retrieved from www.adl.org/media/14643/download

Brilmyer, G. (2018, June 1). Archival assemblages: Applying disability studies' political/relational model to archival description. *Archival Science, 18*(2), 95–118. https://doi.org/10.1007/s10502-018-9287-6.

Brilmyer, G., Gabiola, J., Zavala, J., & Caswell, M. (2019, November 14). Reciprocal archival imaginaries: The shifting boundaries of "community" in community archives. *Archivaria, 88*, 6–48.

Caswell, M., Gabiola, J., Zavala, J., Brilmyer, G., & Cifor, M. (2018, March 1). Imagining transformative spaces: The personal–political sites of community archives. *Archival Science, 18*(1), 73–93. https://doi.org/10.1007/s10502-018-9286-7

Clarke, A. (2005). *Situational Analysis: Grounded Theory After the Postmodern Turn*. New York: Sage Publications.

Crip The Vote. Retrieved from http://cripthevote.blogspot.com/

Garber, M. (2016). Nora Ephron: Prophet of privacy. *The Atlantic*. Retrieved from www.theatlantic.com/entertainment/archive/2016/03/nora-ephron-prophet-of-privacy/475011/

Gardner, C. B. (1995). *Passing by: Gender and public harassment*. Berkeley, CA: University of California Press.

Glaser, A. (2019, November 19). When things go wrong for blind users on Facebook, they go really wrong. *Slate*. Retrieved from https://slate.com/technology/2019/11/facebook-blind-users-no-accessibility.html

Glaser, B. G., & Strauss, A. L. (1967). *The discovery of grounded theory: Strategies for qualitative research*. Chicago, IL: Aldine.

Goffman, E. (1959). *The presentation of self in everyday life*. Garden City, NY: Doubleday.

Goffman, E. (1963). *Stigma: Notes on the management of spoiled identity*. Englewood Cliffs, NJ: Prentice-Hall.

Longmore, P. K. (2003). *Why I burned my book and other essays on disability*. Philadelphia, PA: Temple University Press.

Sadeque, S. (2019, April 29). #WhyDisabledPeopleDropout explores the challenges of being a disabled student. *Daily Dot*. Retrieved from www.dailydot.com/irl/why-disabled-people-drop-out/

Smith, D. E. (1989). *The everyday world as problematic: A feminist sociology*. Lebanon, NH: Northeastern University Press.

Thompson, V., & Wong, A. (2016a, July 26). #GetWokeADA26: Disabled people of color speak out, part one. *Ramp Your Voice*! Retrieved from http://wp.me/p3Ov4P-FA

Thompson, V., & Wong, A. (2016b, July 26). #GetWokeADA26: Disabled people of color speak out, part two. *Ramp Your Voice*! Disability Visibility Project. Retrieved from http://disabilityvisibilityproject.com/2016/07/25/getwokeada26/

Waxman, B. (1994). Up against eugenics: Disabled women's challenge to receive reproductive health services. *Sexuality and Disability, 12*, 155–171. https://doi.org/10.1007/BF02547889

Wong, A. (2020, March). *#Coronavirus and the disability community #COVID –19 #COVID19*. Retrieved from https://wakelet.com/wake/1633ef52-2ade-43a9-b118-50d19f821cb7

Wong, A. *Disability Visibility podcast*. Retrieved from https://disabilityvisibility project.com/podcast-2/

Wong, A. *Disability Visibility Project website*. Retrieved from https://disabilityvisibility project.com/

Wong, A. *Wakelet page*. Retrieved from https://wakelet.com/@AliceWong9697

Zola, I. K. (2003). *Missing pieces: A chronicle of living with a disability*. Philadelphia, PA: Temple University Press.

7 (Re)framing qualitative research as a prickly artichoke

Peeling back the layers of structural ableism within the institutional research process

Holly Pearson and Brianna Dickens

Three, two, one

Remember this melancholy song – "Where Have All the Cowboys Gone?" sung by American singer Paula Cole? It was a popular song in the late '90s – a song about unhappiness and disillusionment with the relationship one is in as one realizes there were never any "cowboys" around to begin with. As the song wraps up, the listener is left with a lingering bitterness. You are probably wondering why we are bringing up this song that was popular over two decades ago. Patience, and trust us, we have a point. The haunting quality of the song and the feeling of unhappiness and disillusionment resonate with our personal inquiries that emerged during our journey as emerging scholars/activists, in particular with the development of our identities as qualitative researchers. As you resume reading this piece, we encourage you to play the song in the background to set the tone.

Within this space, we would like to take a moment – a munching moment upon the historical legacy of qualitative research and its contributions within the context of disability in relations to democracy, sociospatial justice, equity, and social change. Qualitative research reflected the importance of considering the role of one's positionality in shaping one's methods and methodology worldview in counter response/protest to the notion of objectivity of research. Yet, while this may have contributed to significant outcomes or learning moments, the objectification of the participants is a tainted and lingering (problematic) reality that is often swept under the rug.

For instance, with disability there is a long paper trail that documents how research objectified disabled bodyminds (Schalk, 2018) through exclusion of their voices, their experiences, and their needs – while failing to improve the quality of their lives. Essentially, disability is objectified – as neutral nameless "*existence*." In response, a group of scholars urged for the need for emancipatory disability research, a framework that encourages a collective collaboration between researchers and disabled participants throughout the research design and process (Barnes, 2003; Balch & Mertens, 1999; Boxall, 2010; Hall, 2013; Harris, Holmes, & Mertens, 2009; Lester & Nusbaum, 2018; Manning, 2009; Morris, 1992; Oliver, 1992; Price & Kerschbaum, 2016; Ripat & Woodgate, 2011). This framework enables a space to create more inclusive and empowering research practices that shift the notion of ownership. Yet, an underlying problem(s) persist – until *very recently* the process of qualitative research remained unexamined from the lens of disability scholarship, and while emancipatory disability research celebrates inclusive practices with disabled participants, the lived experiences of disabled, d/Deaf,[1] and autistic researchers remains absent or the "unexpected guest."

> What is research?
>
> What constitutes researcher?
>
> What ways can we disrupt the current unspoken ableist assumptions about research/er?
>
> What is research/er methods missing by centering the able body?
>
> What would research/er look like if we centered the disabled body?

In the effort of disrupting the silence around the lived experiences of autistic, Deaf, and disabled researchers, collectively and individually, we explore and address these questions through the form of collective autoethnography. Through our own social locations along with the development of our scholarship, we have, over time, peeled back underlying structural ableism within the notion of research/er in a variety of contexts (e.g., pre-research phase to the write up process, IRB process, and within research methods courses). Each revelation presents an opportunity to munch upon alternative ways of stretching the boundaries of the embodiment of the philosophy and praxis of qualitative research/er.

Furthermore, revelations reflect the significance of addressing the branches of implicit biases and micro/macroaggressions within the context of structural ableism that controls what constitutes research/er. Instead, through our beating hearts, disability becomes central within the dialogue rather than existing on the sideline of presumed incompetence. As a teacher, disability presents alternative ways of engaging with qualitative research/er in the grander scheme of diversity, socio-spatial justice, democracy, inclusion, access, and equity within ivory tower and our communities. Before we dive into a rabbit hole, we wanted to offer insights about who we are, as our lived experiences greatly shape this dialogue that we engage with each other and with you.

Pleased to meet you

Brianna

I identify as autistic and have spent the last seven years trying to find how I fit in or make room for myself in the academy. I spend so much time and energy feeling like a fraud, trying to figure out how to remain true to myself without losing the unsure footing I currently have, in the system that influences so much that goes on in the U.S. school system. My background is in elementary and special education, and I am an educator in both training and interest. Being exposed to disability studies offered me a different way of approaching my work to better the experiences of students that come after me. Throughout my graduate studies I quickly honed in on research as a way to begin to shift what influences knowledge generation and ultimately practice. As a doctoral candidate I spent my time in the academy focusing on research. Much of my time during my doctoral program I was a research assistant for a research institute at my university, as well as a member on a PAR federally funded research study. Reading, thinking, and doing research have been my main focus for the past six years. This chapter is really a conversation in which I share my experiences, alongside my colleague Holly, as an autistic researcher and scholar while situating my experiences within the broader efforts of qualitative researchers.

Holly

The first thing I always make clear when introducing myself is "No, I am not a special educator." "No, I do not teach ASL or Deaf Studies." These are the common misconceptions folks have once I mention that I am Deaf and grew up signing in American Sign Language and communicating in spoken English. Every time, it is extremely fascinating how my career options are reduced to three options. Similarly, with my Asian appearance, without disclosing my disability and deafness, my career options are limited to the following: medical doctor, lawyer, or engineer. In this case, people are perplexed why on earth I pursued degrees in sociology and education. As a disabled/Deaf queer transracial BIPOC adoptee, I am always the oddball wherever I go. This is not necessarily a bad thing, granted it took me time to appreciate insights I gained from navigating multiple boundaries as an oddball, especially intersectional, transdisciplinary, and interdisciplinary lenses. As an oddball, I constantly seek, dream, and create holistic and intimate spaces of radical love and crip time, especially for multiple marginalized disabled communities; thus, critically (re)examining what is research is an act of resistance, resilience, and reclaiming.

Past and current scholarship

Before we dive into our dialogue, we want to ensure folks are familiar with the context that we are building upon as we stretch and massage the current imagination of what is research/er. There have been considerable debates and critiques about research methodologies, in particular with empirical and positivism research due to their emphasis on quantitative approaches along with objectivity, determinism, and generalization (Brown & Strega, 2005; Kovach, 2005; Lofland, 1976; Smith, 1999). The field of qualitative research has branched into multiple strands that offer alternative and/or emancipatory frameworks that shape what constitutes research (e.g., anti-racist research methodologies, decolonizing methodologies, indigenous research, feminist research, queer methodology). For example, indigenous methodologies emphasize cultural protocols, values, and behaviors when considering methodological approaches (Smith, 1999); whereas, anti-racist research methodologies situate those who are minorities within the center of research, while emphasizing the relationship between social oppression and identity construction (Dei, 2005). By drawing from one's own experiences as part of understanding the construction of knowledge, research is about engaging in a critical, reflexive process (Dei, 2005). Alternatively, queer methodologies examine how the queer lens shapes research methods and methodologies (Browne & Nash, 2010). Queer methodologies utilize the queer lens to illustrate the limitations and possibilities within current research methods and methodologies. This brings us to the question of where is disability in the conversation.

Within the field of disability studies, emancipatory disability research was the solution to what changes needed to occur within the research especially dealing with individuals with disabilities (Barnes, 2003; Oliver, 1992). Incorporating an interpretive paradigm, emancipatory disability research illustrates how hegemonic ideologies shape the notion of research and the research process (Oliver, 1992). Emancipatory disability research challenged the positivist paradigm that views disability as a medical and objective state that needs to be fixed due to the common pattern of researching *on* the disabled population, while nixing any need to inquire their input or include them in the research design from the beginning (Barnes, 2003; Boxall, 2010; Munger & Mertens, 2011; Oliver, 1992).

In response, scholars argued that disability research should be a collaborative effort between the researchers and participants with disabilities (Oliver, 1992). In other words, this literature emphasized conducting research *with* rather than *on* those with disabilities. Yes, at that time, this was a shocking revelation. It still continues to be an issue, unfortunately. This involves including the voices and perspectives of those with disabilities as part of the research process in a collaborative manner that emphasizes trust and mutual respect while being critically mindful of one's own biases and addressing the power differential between the two groups (Manning, 2009; Oliver, 1992). Emancipatory disability research has the potential to empower those with disabilities by creating possibilities of ownership in their participation in the research process and facilitating a deeper understanding of the relationship between self and society (Barnes, 2003; Morris, 1992; Oliver, 1992; Ripat & Woodgate, 2011). Since then, scholars have attempted to establish more inclusive and empowering research practices that enable those with disabilities to not only be a part of the research process, but also structured a space where they or disability has a voice within the research process across multiple platforms (e.g., conferences, articles, book chapters, podcasts, etc.) and disciplines (e.g., English, sociology, education, etc.).

As Deaf, disabled, and autistic researchers/scholars/activists, here is where we pick up the conversation thread. Returning to the song "Where Have All the Cowboys Gone?" we inquire where the insights of disabled, autistic, mad, and d/Deaf researchers are. Similarly to growing up with no role models who reflected our identities and realities, we desire communities and spaces that recognize and *get it* – what it is like to be multiply marginalized in a toxic, ableist, homophobic, racist, sexist, and classist society that has viewed disabled bodyminds as lesser than from day one. We crave breathing realms of *access intimacy* and *interdependence* (Mingus, 2017a).

Swish swish, swirling all the favors

To begin our munching, the following questions served as a prompt to ignite, jog, and/or trigger feelings, thoughts, and unfinished inquiries:

What does it mean to center disability in qualitative inquiry to you?
As an X, Y, Z (how you identify yourself), how do you feel, see, interpret, define, reconstruct, etc., the notion of research/researcher?
In what ways can we disrupt the current unspoken ableist assumptions about research/er?
What are research/er methods missing by centering the able body?
What would research/er look like if we centered the disabled body?

Inner turmoil in journey in research (Brianna)

My journey in the academy and in becoming a researcher really got its start during the height of a nationally covered court case about a sexual relationship involving a man who types to communicate. Competency, intelligence, and what counts as communication were central to the case. Also central to the case was facilitated communication (FC), a method of communication that has been under scrutiny since its inception. During this time, understandably, the research surrounding the communication method was brought to the forefront. This case and the response to it by the disability community and the research community (particularly those doing research about the communication method) was a major focus during the first year of my PhD program. While the response from the larger disability community was to center disability, competency, and intelligence, highlighting the need to shift how we think about competency and consent, the response that I experienced from the research and FC community was different. The response from the FC community and research community, as I know, was to continue to work, following closely to "best practices" as determined by the existing research and to adhere closely to "qualitative standards" in current and future work.

This was my introduction to research in any substantive way. On the disability community side, a centering of disability, on the academy side, a centering of the current ableist notions of knowledge and knowledge creation. Rather than centering disability, this response centered current, traditional qualitative research, and an able-bodied perspective. I am not critiquing the response as I understand and respect where it came from; I merely use this to illustrate my experiences in research during my time in the academy. The tensions surrounding the court case and responses to it offer a larger, more visible example of the tensions and turmoil I felt within myself as I worked to establish myself as a scholar and researcher.

I spent the majority of the last six years thinking about what it means to be a researcher. First, trying to center the able-bodied norm, even within myself. Trying to push away my true self, my ways of knowing and being and trying to fit in, quickly crashing and burning. Then, running into barrier after barrier, as I brought myself, my ways of knowing and being into my work. There is vulnerability that is required to centering disability in research as a disabled researcher that I had to learn to embrace. I often refer back to the court case mentioned earlier as it was so much a part of my journey into research and to remind myself of the harm done when disability is not centered, who ultimately gets hurt and left behind. While efforts were made to try and protect individuals through the centering of the academy and traditional qualitative research, those efforts ultimately upheld the system of oppression that the academy is built upon. There are systems and structures in the academy that are in place and define what knowledge is and is not, who can be knowledgeable and who cannot.

Many of these systems and structures, just as the responses to the court case by the FC community, are in place in the name of protection. Consent procedures that are aimed at protecting children and individuals with intellectual and/or developmental disabilities limit individuals' abilities to be a part of research and to be researchers. There are also systems for research dissemination such as top tier journal requirements, job security being tied to publishing, and academic writing standards with requirements that often force ableist notions of knowledge creation and sharing. In centering disability, all of these core systems come under scrutiny, and become de-stabilized, bringing with it hope for change in the knowledge creation process and power.

Twisting myself into knots: psychic mindduckery (Holly)

Engaging in a "restless reflective" (Titchkosky, 2011) is to holistically reexamine taken for granted background expectancies in everyday life. The concept of background expectancies provides a means to tease out taken for granted rules, procedures, and societal norms that influence our behaviors in everyday processes. Because they are taken for granted, one fails to critically consider the implications or perpetuations within those actions or ideologies (Titchkosky, 2006). "Restless reflective" is to be resilient and to resist by exposing and disrupting dominant positivist ways of knowing, understanding, and interpreting (Titchkosky, 2011). "Restless reflexive" started in the required qualitative research courses for graduate work, which involved practicing the basic staples: interviewing, participant observations, and transcribing (along with coding and analyzing the text). Every time I went to pieces, because it was an incredibly ableist experience. I always find it problematic when texts imply that to be a solid researcher center around the ability to ask *good* questions, listen, observe, and read. Here are two past scenarios to center my munching around.

Sitting in a local high school classroom to observe the interactional process among the teacher, teaching staff, and the students. The teacher was teaching a lesson that required students to engage with her and each other, so there was considerable verbal dialogue. During the lesson, the teacher came over and encouraged me to walk around and interact with students, while whispering information about the classroom and the students. I did not understand what was said due to deafness and the noise level in the classroom. At the time, I just nodded as if I understood, and continued to sit and observe the students as they worked on their assignments. As I continued to observe, the sounds from multiple dialogues washed over me as waves of blurred distorted sounds. To compensate for my hearing loss, I jotted down notes that I could visually see and interpret and attempted to lip-read the dialogue between students. By the end, I was exhausted from being hypervigilant.

Visualizing my past interviewing experiences, there appears to be this "typical" setup: a room that is quiet, and well-lit with enough space for the interviewer and the interviewee. A quiet room is one with little to no ambient white noise interference such as an air conditioning turned on. A well-lit room enables me to read lips and *understand* more of the conversation. Not being able to lip-read makes it extremely difficult for me to understand conversations when I need to rely solely on hearing. Minimizing the presence of other people minimizes background noise that interferes with my ability to hear and minimizes visual distraction as well. My visual abilities compensate for my hearing loss by being extra sensitive to movement, which can be extremely distracting. A significant degree of hidden labor goes into the setup to enable myself to engage as a hearing person.

In both situations, I felt conflicted in my participation in masking or rendering disability invisible and perpetuating neutrality by upholding the dominant ideologies of what constitutes research/er. Conceptualizing research as a form of social interaction allows one to see how interviewing and participant observation play a role in shaping meaning and assumptions about the research and the researcher within the context of able-bodied and disabled. In the interviewing process, the two parties are co-constructing what constitutes research/er. By masking my disability, I lost the opportunity to counter the hegemonic notion of an able-bodied researcher. Additionally, dominant notions of research methods were perpetuated by my efforts to interview in an oral and listening manner, rather than utilizing services such as Real Time captioning or an interpreter.

Returning to the methodological texts, something as simple as an interview screamed ableism. Messages such as the interviewer needs to "be respectful and courteous, and offer few questions and advice" (Creswell, 2007, p. 134), along with being a good listener who has strong interpersonal skills (Rossman & Rallis, 2012) are extremely problematic. Failing to critically reexamine the assumed qualitative methods (e. g., participant observation, interviewing, and transcribing) is to perpetuate a monoculture of what constitutes research/er along with the erasure of alternative ways of thinking and engaging (Shiva, 1993).

The absence of alternative ways of engaging – such as discussion of how to navigate interviews with hearing participants in ASL with an ASL interpreter who revoices what you are saying, conducting participant observation as a Deaf Asian female in a predominantly hearing white institution, or a BIPOC transgender individual who wants to conduct research on white supremacist attitudes in a small town that strongly embraces Catholic homophobia – is problematic, period. When raising these kinds of questions, often, blank stares are the outcome. An additional problematic response stems from the assumptions that folks will or should address research questions/topics that *naturally* align with one's identities and lived experiences. It becomes problematic when a person in power, an authority figure, pigeonholes or boxes in an emerging scholar into a particular topic *just because*. In both cases, no further discussion takes place – no pushing the boundaries of what is research/er. No centering, weaving in complexity, intersections, or radical love of holistic resistance and resilience.

Breathing together

In this moment we are still digesting and molding our sense of what it means to center disability and how our identities and lived experiences continue to shape our understanding of research/er. A few thoughts emerge:

How can centering disability in qualitative inquiry not only infuse socio-social justice and disability justice principles, but also facilitate environment(s) where disabled scholars thrive rather than "co"-existing in survivor mode in toxic landscapes? This involves recognizing how forced intimacy flourishes across such landscapes. Forced intimacy, as Mingus (2017b) explains, is where disabled people often have to exhibit extreme vulnerability in order to exist and matter in a hostile environment that is built for a particular person – aka the Ken doll. Forced intimacy is ensnared among the roots of qualitative inquiry. To mold our bodyminds, to mask our disabilities, to conform to qualify in order to be seen as a *competent* researcher is traumatic and triggering, especially when multiply marginalized bodyminds grow up knowing they are different, knowing they are not normal, while being "forced" (aka encouraged) to strive to be as normal as the ideal. To be able to see, hear, talk, make eye contact, or stand still are potential, yet ableist, indicators of a competent researcher. How to cease this cycle is the question.

Returning to the lyrics of "Where Have All the Cowboys Gone?" to begin dreaming of systemic changes across the educational landscape, we, ourselves need to recognize the knowledge that we have to offer is extremely valuable and necessary in these kinds of conversations. It is evident of a need for diverse perspectives in qualitative inquiry, and has been done so by queer, anti-racist, post-colonial, feminist, and indigenous scholars. Yet, where are the disabled scholars? Where is the centering of disability in research? It is time for disabled scholars, especially those who embodied multiply marginalized embodiments, and who are most vulnerable, to reclaim and take ownership of research through creation, community care, and radical love. This is when we begin to thrive rather than survive.

This involves recognizing how the pursuit of knowledge and the construction of knowledge involve multiple layers of ideologies and practices (Dei, 2005; Smith, 1999). To raise not the question of "who the knowledge is created for," but rather "how it is created and for what purposes" (Smith, 1999, p. 4), is moving towards social justice, equity, and empowerment, which also involves "challenge(ing) the norms of what it means to know and how we come to know, imagination is essential" (Osei-Kofi, 2013, p. 139). It is the space(s) of marginalization that enables an alternative way of interpreting the taken for granted notions that entwine with personal experiences (Brown & Strega, 2005; Smith, 1999). The space of marginalization(s) are where one can resist by engaging in the activity of researching back, a process similar to writing back or talking back (Smith, 1999).

Yet, thriving involves vulnerability. How can we breathe together? Infuse love and compassion from within? Facilitate community care? Undigest the hegemonic ideologies of white supremacy, homophobia, transphobia, sexism, classism, and ableism? It is not fair to ask the very folks, those who are positioned at these margins, to stand up alone and resist. To create, to only have their work co-opted or ignored. Yes, it is important to facilitate a growing network of disabled scholars who take ownership in centering disability in scholarship, but also the very individuals who have power, privilege, financial security, and tenure need to also shake up the system by working with disabled scholars, citing, bringing in, and compensating for them their time. If you do not understand what we are talking about, take a moment and look back at your educational journey – how many of your teachers were disabled? How many of your role models were disabled? How many of your peers were disabled? How many of your administrators were disabled? Do not count the ones who teach in conventional fields that are deemed acceptable for disabled bodyminds such as special education, inclusive education, deaf studies, etc. How many can you think of off the top of your head who were disrupting and defying the intersectional ableist expectations? This is precisely the very issue here. To ask us to create and pour our souls and hearts into this movement without systemic change is setting us up to fail, to be disregarded, or to be co-opted, while allowing the cycle of institutional violence to flourish unchecked.

Thriving is also about collective accountability. For us, who occupy multiple roles and identities in the disabled community, this involves undigesting the toxic, dehumanizing knowledge that we all were force-fed to believe is true. Unpacking does not happen overnight, as we know. We spent x number of years digesting both consciously and unconsciously. It is not until much later in our journey that we encounter amazing folks who challenge the hegemonic ideologies and nudge us to critically (re)examine within. Holding each other in a safe breathing space are amazing act(s) of accountability in the spirit of love and compassion. To (re)learn how to love ourselves, to be vulnerable, and to be able to connect with kindred spirits. To love ourselves is to realize that each one of us has something to offer, and each other's insights are critical in order to cease the vicious cycle of oppression in one another. Our presence is and will always be an act of disruption and resistance.

For those who are allies, we encourage you to do the same: to critically (re)examine within, to unpack hegemonic ideologies that unconsciously and consciously encourage you to stratify certain bodyminds over others. While there is little data about the numbers of disabled bodyminds in higher education, taking a moment to look back and think of how many mad, d/ Deaf, autistic, and disabled scholar/activists you had an opportunity to engage with, especially in positions of power, and how this reflects a painfully honest reality of the toxicity that flows freely, with zero accountability, across educational landscapes. That is the easy step. The hard work is continuing to work towards structuring equity and just praxis, which involves intentionally and strategically conspiring. This involves shifting resources, privilege, and leverage. This may involve taking a step back, stop talking for us, or just listening. This is a quest, not a damn sprint. Do not pick the easiest task such as hosting a disability awareness day. We live and breathe our realities and identities day in and out. We do not have the privilege to remove ourselves from a particular situation or to stop being our very fabric of our existence. To do nothing is to be complicit in upholding violence, in all forms.

It is also important to not make the error that commonly occurs when bringing disability into the conversation from the sidelines. Often disability is engaged in isolation. This is problematic as it reinforces the false notion that disability exists in isolation. Disability is deeply entwined with race, class, gender, sexuality, religion, and citizenship. Therefore, while it is important to develop deeper, more complex conversations that center disability in the conversation, it is vital to break the mold of isolating disability by incorporating an intersectional lens, by bringing in a diverse array of voices/lived experiences. From here, this creates the possibility of building a rooted legacy where future disabled scholars from all walks of life can resume building and pushing the boundaries of qualitative inquiry.

Returning to the "beginning"

Similar to the disability studies' conceptualization of disability, the lens of disability reframes research methods as social, cultural, political, economic, ideological, and discursive social phenomena (Davis, 1995; Titchkosky, 2006). In this chapter we take space to engage in a critical reflective process both individually and together to better understand the construction of knowledge and the process of research (Dei, 2005). We take a moment to breathe together, to try to digest and unpack our experiences as disabled researchers and activists, working within the ableist structure and system that is the academy. We offer our own munchings in hopes of working to peel back the oppressive layers of the artichoke that is the academy and in hopes of supporting the work to use the lens of disability to reframe research methods.

> *Where is my happiness?*
> *Where is my existence?*
> *Where is my space(s) to heal?*
> *Where have all the disabled communities gone?*

We are here. We matter. We are no longer asking for permission. Stop trying to eradicate our existence. No longer will we continue to squeeze ourselves into what constitutes "normal." Cease squeezing ourselves into a mismatched peg hole that was designed by folks who can never fully understand multiply marginalized existence (Mingus, 2017a). Stop the vicious cycle of unhappiness and disillusionment. Instead, we can intentionally choose to channel our spoons towards collectively infusing radical love and interdependence within (re)creating spaces with our communities. Let's breathe, scream, cry, laugh, and sigh together. You are not alone.

We end the chapter offering a few questions for researchers to consider as they design and carry out qualitative research studies:

1   How can we work to redefine who counts as a knowledge contributor, taking into consideration what this means in ableist systems and structures, specifically centering multiply marginalized communities? (To begin thinking about this involves us (re)examining how we are maintaining and upholding systemic ableism.)

2   Situated within the context of neoliberalism and expectations of what it means to be a "prolific" researcher/scholar, how can you shift your research study and pedagogy so that it does not co-opt and further marginalize multiply marginalized disabled communities, and perpetuate the current, systemic violence cycle? (To respond involves pondering upon your relationship with multiply marginalized communities and how one is complicit in maintaining the current systemic violence.)

3   How can we make space for disabled scholars (d/Deaf, neurodivergent, mad, autistic, etc.), especially those who embody multiply marginalized, and who are most vulnerable, to reclaim and take ownership of research through creation, community care, and radical love? (To answer this question about how we can make space involves us contemplating the relationship between interdependence and radical love.)

4   How have you carved out ways of cripping your research so it is infused with self-love and community care? In other words, how does self-love and community care shape your research design? (To answer this question involved us grappling with and problematizing what is self-love and community care.)

Note

1 Uppercase "D" in Deaf applies to folks who identify as culturally deaf, while lower case "d" in deaf is for folks who have various degrees of hearing loss, but may not have a strong sense of Deaf identity or culture.

References

Balch, G. I., & Mertens, D. M. (1999). Focus group design and group dynamics: Lessons from the deaf and hard of hearing participants. *American Journal of Evaluation, 20*(2), 265–277. https://doi.org/10.1177/109821409902000208

Barnes, C. (2003). What a difference a decade makes: Reflections on doing "emancipatory" disability research. *Disability & Society, 18*(1), 3–17. https://doi.org/10.1080/713662197

Boxall, K. (2010). Research ethics committees and the benefits of involving people with profound and multiple learning disabilities. *British Journal of Learning Disabilities, 39*(1), 173–180. https://doi.org/10.1111/j.1468-3156.2010.00645.x

Brown, L., & Strega, S. (2005). Transgressive possibilities. In L. Brown & S. Strega (Eds.), *Research as resistance: Critical, indigenous, and anti-oppressive approaches* (pp. 1–17). Toronto, Ontario: Canadian Scholars' Press/Women's Press.

Browne, K., & Nash, C. J. (Eds.). (2010). *Intersecting queer theories and social science research.* Burlington, VT: Ashgate Publishing Company.

Creswell, J. W. (2007). *Qualitative inquiry and research design: Choosing among five approaches* (2nd ed.). Thousand Oaks, CA: Sage Publication Inc.

Davis, L. J. (1995). *Enforcing normalcy: Disability, deafness, and the body.* New York: Verso.

Dei, G. J. S. (2005). Critical issues in anti-racist research methodologies. In G. J. S. Dei & G. S. Johal (Eds.), *Critical issues in anti-racist research methodologies* (pp. 1–27). New York: Peter Lang Publishing, Inc.

Hall, S. A. (2013). Including people with intellectual disabilities in qualitative research. *Journal of Ethnographic & Qualitative Research, 7*(3), 128–142.

Harris, R., Holmes, H. M., & Mertens, D. M. (2009). Research ethics in sign language communities. *Sign Language Studies, 9*(2), 104–131. https://doi.org/10.1353/sls.0.0011

Kovach, M. (2005). Emerging from the margins: Indigenous methodologies. In L. Brown & S. Strega (Eds.), *Research as resistance: Critical, indigenous, and anti-oppressive approaches* (pp. 19–36). Toronto, Ontario: Canadian Scholars' Press/Women's Press.

Lester, J. N., & Nusbaum, E. (2018). "Reclaiming" disability in critical qualitative research: Introduction to the special issue. *Qualitative Inquiry, 24*(1), 3–7. https://doi.org/10.1177/1077800417727761

Lofland, J. (1976). *Doing social life: The qualitative study of human interaction in natural settings.* New York: John Wiley & Sons, Inc.

Manning, C. (2009). "My memory's back!" Inclusive learning disability research using ethics, oral history and digital storytelling. *British Journal of Learning Disabilities, 38*(1), 160–167. https://doi.org/10.1111/j.1468-3156.2009.00567

Mingus, M. (2017a, April 12). *Access intimacy, interdependence and disability justice* [Blog post]. Retrieved from https://leavingevidence.wordpress.com/2017/04/12/access-intimacy-interdependence-and-disability-justice/

Mingus, M. (2017b, August 6). *Forced intimacy: An ableist norm* [Blog post]. Retrieved from https://leavingevidence.wordpress.com/2017/08/06/forced-intimacy-an-ableist-norm/

Morris, J. (1992). Personal and political: A feminist perspective on researching physical disability. *Disability, Handicap & Society, 7*(2), 157–166.

Munger, K. M., & Mertens, D. M. (2011). Conducting research with the disability community: A rights-based approach. *New Directions for Adults and Continuing Education, 2011*(132), 23–33. https://doi.org/10.1002/ace/428

Oliver, M. (1992). Changing the social relations of research production. *Disability, Handicap & Society, 7*(2), 101–114.

Osei-Kofi, N. (2013). The emancipatory potential of art-based research for social justice. *Equity & Excellence in Education, 46*(1), 135–149. Retrieved from http://doi.org/10.1080/10665684.2013.750202

Price, M., & Kerschbaum, S. (2016). Stories of methodology: Interviewing sideways, crooked, and crip. *Canadian Journal of Disability Studies, 5*(3), 18–56. https://doi.org/10.15353/cjds.v5i3.295

Ripat, J. D., & Woodgate, R. L. (2011). Locating assistive technology within an emancipatory disability research framework. *Technology and Disability, 23*, 87–92. https://doi.org/10.3233/TAD-2011-0315

Rossman, G. B., & Rallis, S. F. (2012). *Learning in the field: An introduction to qualitative research* (3rd ed.). Thousand Oaks, CA: Sage Publication, Inc.

Schalk, S. (2018). *Bodyminds reimagined: (Dis)ability, race, and gender in Black women's speculative fiction.* Durham, NC: Duke University Press.

Shiva, V. (1993). *Monocultures of the mind: Perspectives on biodiversity and biotechnology.* London, UK: Zed Books Ltd.

Smith, L. T. (1999). *Decolonizing methodologies: Research and indigenous people.* New York: Palgrave.

Titchkosky, T. (2006). *Disability, self and society.* Toronto, Canada: University of Toronto Press.

Titchkosky, T. (2011). *The question of access: Disability, space, meaning.* Toronto, Canada: University of Toronto Press.

Index

CPSIA information can be obtained
at www.ICGtesting.com
Printed in the USA
LVHW011157240723
753032LV00030B/97